Humanising Workplace -Pathway to HR Management

Dr. Nitin H. Deshpande

Publisher: ChiRaNi Prakashan, Pune in collaboration with Pranav Jere

Front Page: Pranav Jere

Copyright© Dr. Nitin H. Deshpande

ISBN: 9781078011112

Date of release: August 25, 2019

Edition: First

Dedicated to the Memory of,

Late Shri V. V. Deshpande

Who inspired by Theory in Ethical Management

Late Shri Suresh Hundre

Who inspired by Practice in Ethical Management

CONTENTS

My Work! My Words!! 7

Industrial Scenario in India 9

Maharashtrian Saints and Their Contribution Towards Societal Development 18

Biography of Saint Dnyaneshwar 28

Biography of Saint Tukaram 39

Biography of Samarth Ramdas Swami 48

Shrimat Bhagvad Gita 61

Dnyaneshwari (Bhavarth Dipika) 90

Tukaram Gatha 104

Dasbodh 114

Similarity in Teachings and Writings of Samarth Ramdas and Jagad Guru Tukaram Maharaj 143

Few Examples of Similarity Between Teachings of Samarth Ramdas Swami and Modern Management Gurus 154

Linkage Between Saints and HR 162

Annexures 169

Validation 206

My Work! My Words!!

Humanising work place is the primary task of HR function, which somehow HR fraternity has hardly succeeded till date despite best of brains and technological support! Of all the resources, human beings are the most critical and at the same time delicate to deal with. The tag is "handle with care."

All these years, I was also searching for some sustainable answer. Trigger came from Daily Sakal, when I read an article "Business Ashram" - a corporate experiment by late Shri Suresh Hundre at M/s Polyhydron Pvt. Ltd; Belgaum who firmly believed in "Temple of Ethics."

Then the journey was simple. I visited thrice to meet him, to understand the experiences since 1982 and success story of Polyhydron. Wrote a no. of research papers and realised that sustainable solutions for HR issues are from this soil only, since the problems are also home grown.

Books by Dr. Anand Nadkarni, Shri Sudhir Nirgudkar and Guruji (Shri G. Narayana) and many others firmed my belief in the work by Shrimat Bhagvad Gita, Dnyaneshwari, Tukaram Gatha and Dasbodh for corporate solutions. If these literary books can influence our personal life for so many centuries, then it will be wiser to apply their teachings and writings to professional life as well. The attempts got supported by some likeminded people and the research reached its logical conclusion.

This book is based on my research for Ph.D. and subsequent validation through experimentation in selected enterprises.

We could create couple of success stories both in Manufacturing and Service sectors.
Today, at the release of this book, a new experimentation possibility and opportunity is awaiting.

It works, I am convinced! It's HR fraternity's time to take a call!!

Dr. Nitin H. Deshpande

CHAPTER 1

Industrial Scenario in India

In India, the enterprises have been classified broadly into two categories: (i) Manufacturing; and (ii) Those engaged in providing/rendering of services. Both categories of enterprises have been further classified into micro, small and medium enterprises based on their investment in plant and machinery (for manufacturing enterprises) or on equipment (in case of enterprises providing or rendering services).

Organisations of today are facing a set of new problems in terms of Customers, Competition, Technology and Government legislations. Having global players around, the scenario is truly change driven and is raising questions of survival and sustenance.

No. of HR initiatives and experiments have been tried and tested in the past to address business challenges. Many western philosophies, concepts have been installed in our organisations. Indian organisations have tried to follow well-known western management gurus and replicate their success formulae with or without customisation. All these attempts were successful to some extent and benefitted those organisations.

The employees' need for meaningful existence is prominent these days. Employees are no longer happy with professional success or material gains alone. Secondly, corporate leadership is looking for newer ways to motivate employees and find out innovative solutions.

On this backdrop, it was felt whether we can try our own solutions to address our HR issues?

Many western philosophies, concepts have been installed in our organisations. Indian Organisation have tried to follow well-known western management gurus and adapt to their formulae. All this brought success to some extent and benefits to those organisations.

On eastern front, it is distinctly visible that we have tradition of wisdom for last so many centuries. Generations of common, ordinary people in Maharashtra have been transformed by the teachings and writings of saints. They have offered better quality of personal life. Even illiterate villager in Maharashtra knows Dnyaneshwari, Gatha and Dasbodh. All these find their origins in Bhagvad Gita. These writings are in poetry form, typically verses (Shloka) which are easier to remember and through their chanting there has been impact on the thinking and behaviour of common people. Some visible and proven effects on personal life can be summarised as- No smoking, No non vegetarian food, Speaking truth, no consumption of alcohol, observing fast, engaged in spiritual reading and trying to practice it in day-to-day life, respect to family traditions and culture.

In his famous book "Dasbodh' Saint Ramdas explains all management principles right from running a home neatly to concepts such as waste management, cost control etc in the form of 'bodh' (advice).

Today, we have coined a word "employee" who has both personal and professional life. These have overlapping effects on each other and the two compartments cannot be separated. If on personal front, these simple and easy to follow principles can be practiced, then can these be applied to professional life?

The effects can be checked on some aspects of professional life. For example-

Reducing negative habits at work place, enhancing punctuality, honesty, attitudinal changes and approach towards work (Duty is of prime importance), Work Commitment (absolute involvement of mind and body), productivity, good interpersonal relations, achievement motivation.

The spiritual literature has shown path to handle variety of situations, problems in the past. It is capable of enlightening our path even in modern day situations, with solutions from our own soil.

According to a survey conducted by Confederation of Indian Industries, 20% of Medium and 80% of Small sized businesses have no HR Department. Increasing attention of HRM in SMEs is a comparatively recent phenomenon. HR Researchers have largely ignored the SMEs even though smaller companies could be fruitful subjects due to diversity in their management practices. For SMEs to ensure long term success in the market, it is crucial to have systematic HR Practices. Indian SMEs can always learn from the big players and address their HR challenges through proper customisation. For them the two biggest challenges, over and above others are competent work force and recruiting the right talent.

In the knowledge-driven society of today, human resource provides the cutting edge to organisations, as all other resources are equally accessible. Hence challenges before HR are-

- Attracting and retaining talent
- Enhancement in current level of productivity
- Bringing about desirable changes in attitude/behaviour of employees (Mindset change)
- Development and preparing manpower for tomorrows challenges (Management of Change)
- To appeal and awaken inner self, to justify one's way of work and to make employees fit, so that they offer their best to the organisation to accomplish the organisational goals.
- Small and Medium scale organisations even today are not in a position to have a full-fledged HR department in place. Mostly these are run by the owners, who also happen to be HR heads for their organisations. Their philosophy largely governs their organisations. The entire HR function has hardly any structured, well written policies, documentation and focused development interventions. The work force is not stable and attrition rate is high.

HRD Philosophies and Concepts: The Indian Perspective

Organisations in India need to change fundamentally if they are to be globally competitive. This will imply changes in the way people relate to the organisation and to each other as they go about the business of achieving the business objectives. In this context HRD emerges as a critical and strategic variable in the life of a transforming organisation.

HRD is viewed differently by different people. For several years it is a more misunderstood concept than a rightly understood one. In many ways there is nothing new in this concept. In some other way there are many new things new. The notion of Human Resources Development has changed from just maintenance to that of enabling and empowering employees to grow to the limits of their capabilities. If one interprets HRD as a process of learning, growth, maturation and continuous development of an individual, there is nothing new. It is as old as the existence of human being although how human beings learn, grow and develop is a sought after subject by psychologists, business thinkers and researchers. Especially in the last three decades, HRD has evolved as a concept to denote much more than what it was perceived earlier. It came from the tradition of "Training" in the west and as a philosophy in the east (especially Japan and India). HRD also meant creation of a climate in the organisation that promotes the utilisation and development of new competencies so as to provide better quality of life. Culture building became a part of the agenda of HRD.

World Bank and several other UN agencies have brought out the importance of HRD. The concept of Human Development promoted by the United Nations Development Programme (UNDP) is very much synonymous to HRD.

In order to build the vision of HRD at a larger scale, we should understand from the leaders of business organisations and thinking managers, as to how they see HRD.

Human Resource function with the brain and a heart distinguishes it from all other resources. Own individual characteristics stemming from the personality and personal traits make every individual different from another. That makes it the most fundamental and substantive input in any enterprise. The stability of an enterprise apart from financial viability is conditioned by the relationship between the owner and the employees of the enterprise.

To provide the quality of human endeavour, it is not merely necessary to impart right training, but also to create an environment where workmen are not merely allocated work and treated as just another resource, but self respect and dignity as an individual has to respected and protected. The organisation has to create an environment where individuals and teams are provided with an opportunity to move towards realisation of their potential. Dissent has to surface as an indicator of openness and freedom of expression, which has to be attended to rather than suppressed.

HRD has to bring about a positive change in the work ethos, which would support the efforts of making Indian Industry, market oriented and internationally competitive. Due to multiplication of job opportunities, HRD in any organisation has to create a stable nucleus of loyal and dedicated people, which in itself is a daunting task but a life-time opportunity as well. HRD is a common sense approach to deal with human beings which is translated into scientific thinking of "why people behave the way they behave?" Although HRD is playing an important role, its future is slow due to immense diversity. Organisations are slowly realising that by creating a culture that values all employees, encourages and rewards high performance, continuous improvement, foster teamwork through empowering individuals can achieve and retain their market leadership in chosen product/ service segments. This climate has to ensure that the individuals would become members of synergic groups at the work situation by sustaining human touch despite size of the organisation. Individuals only decide how to use their own capabilities so success of HRD lies in people practicing it. Organisation needs people and people should also belong to their organisation.

There is a shift in paradigm taking place all over the globe. People are frustrated with the current reality of chasing only materialistic goals and economic success. There is a new yarning for universal holistic management. The unipolarity is realising the dream "Vasudeva Kutumbakam." The role of HRD is to create a foundation for this new paradigm to operate. Its biggest aim is to bring about a change in the mindset and create competencies needed to match the new mind set. This will call for massive investment in training and organisations are gearing up for that, which is a good sign.

HRD must also redesign its own role to keep itself in consonance with the changing scenario. HRD has to facilitate the shift from the traditional style of managing which is predominantly individual and result oriented to a style which is group and process oriented.

The investment made in HRD have long gestation period and therefore it takes a long time to get the results for which the management needs to demonstrate patience.

CHAPTER 2

Maharashtrian Saints and Their Contribution Towards Societal Development

In Mahabharata there is a dialogue between Dharma (Yudhisthir) and Yaksha. A simple question Yaksha asks him- "Dharma raj, Ka Dick? (What is Direction?)" The immediate reply comes from Dharma- "Santo Dick! (Saints means Direction.)"

Bhagwat Dharma says – Saints are society oriented Bhaktas. They have two tasks- Bhakti through Namsmarana (chanting of divine name) and secondly uniting people. Chanting develops inwardness. This is first step. Over a period of time such inward Bhakta starts working for society. The transactions between these two stages take place at two levels. Such evolved personality according to Bhagwat

Dharma is "Saint." In short saint is for society but the basis is purification of self.

The first visible impact on society as envisioned by Saints is upliftment of level and quality of life of people. In the process of devotion, uniting people does not become obstacle for saints. In fact it is external dimension of Saint's sadhana. This is not choice but it is mandatory for Saints. Saints must move constantly, hence the tradition of Vari started.

According to Yogi Arbindo "Human mind is miniature form of super mind. Our mind constantly attempts to attain this super status like a water body. Maya, grid on the other hand try to pull it down. The upward movement of mind is constantly inspired and motivated by company of saints."

Saints have always tried to create good will, reduce power of evil and reinforcing faith on human values. They have always tried to ensure that divine energy in human beings is intensified, create balance between Sattava, Rajas and Tamasi gunas/sutras. Through own behaviour, saints demonstrated how to overcome personal evils.

Saints taught us through their literature that we must always and only listen to our inner voice, which gives new and better dimension to our present life. Saints are media of divine inspirations. They are selfless; they try to build a society through their positive efforts. Saints constantly remind us about our duties, create concrete foundation of positivity, insist upon good behaviour and attempt for assertive society.

The route suggested by Saints is three fold.

Prabodhan …….. Prayatna……… Pratyaya

(Enlightenment……Efforts……..Experience)

Indian minds always feel that Saints always accompany mankind and they are there through their writings and teachings. Saints practice dharma as highlighted in Vedas and become role model for us.

Samarth Ramdas in praise of saints in Dasbodh says "saints are the resort of spiritual life and through whose goodness secret knowledge of God becomes known to the world. By remaining in the company of saints, that thing which is very difficult to reach, which is very rare and can be got by great luck, is easily available. The Absolute thing is gradually realised in the company of saints by personal experience. Saints are the abode of joy and happiness incarnate. The saints are the primary source of all contentment. Freedom finds rest in the saints, they are the fulfilment of the fulfillments or we can say that they are the fruit of devotion. Saints are the place of pilgrimage of religion; saints are the holy containers of Reality. They are the sacred place of pure piety. Trance finds a temple in the consciousness of saints.

Saints are the storehouse of discernment and discretion, or they can be called the mother's home for complete liberation. Saints are the finality of truth. They are the victory of life fulfilment. Meeting them is the auspicious time of final achievement. The saints are really noble who have the riches of Freedom as their glory and they have made rich kings out of many poor people. Those who are powerful, benevolent, charitable are not able to give that wisdom which the saints give us. Such is the greatness of saints and any simile given is inadequate for them, by whose grace the realisation of GOD becomes possible."

The Marathi poet-saints are an exception to the general rule that Indian devotional literature shows little awareness of the prevailing social conditions. The Marathi "saints", both implicitly and explicitly, questioned the elitist monopoly of spiritual knowledge and privilege embodied in the caste hierarchy.

They were strongly egalitarian and preached universal love and compassion. They trusted their native language, Marathi, more than Sanskrit of the scriptures or the erudite commentaries thereon. They made language a form of shared religion and religion a shared language. It is they who helped to bind the Marathas together against the Mughals on the basis not of any religious ideology but a territorial cultural identity. Their egalitarian legacy continues into modern times with Jotiba Phule, Vitthal Ramji Shinde, Chattrapati Shahu, Sayaji Rao Gaekwad and B.R. Ambedkar - all outstanding social reformers and activists. The gamut of Bhakti poetry has amazing depth, width and range: it is hermitic, esoteric, cryptic, mystical; it is sensuous, lyrical, deeply emotional, devotional, it is vivid, graphic, frank, direct; it is ironic, sarcastic, critical; it is colloquial, comic, absurd; it is imaginative, inventive, experimental; it is intense, angry, assertive and full of protest.

The journey began in 13th century and the conviction still continues. Saints showed us path to life and also life after death. The language used by saints to lead to spiritual and social upliftment brought them close to common man. Their thought process ultimately led to realisation of truth. Once the saints got this realisation, they took the responsibility to lead others towards the destination. Dharma is an important organ of society and it is the faith of ordinary people. To bring knowledge of Dharma to the doorsteps of deprived common, illiterate people, saints used Prakrit(Marathi) as medium of their expressions. At times they chose similes, sometimes poetry to pin point wrong traits in human beings and showed correct path to the world. Since both knowledge and Bhakti are complementary to each other, Saints accepted combination of thoughts and emotions. Saints are basically human beings so they have seen and experienced all shades of life. This enabled them to reduce gap between reality and ideals. Saints always proposed inclusive growth. Respecting opinions of others and respecting religion of others is the visionary thought which saints propagated through their writings and teachings. They brought change in the history of Maharashtra through humanity, equality. The tripod is best described as Sat-chit-ananda.

The tradition of the Marathi saints conceives the role of a poet in its own unique way, which has deep ethno-poetic significance.

Bhakti (Devotion) is founded in a spirit of universal fellowship. Its basic principle is sharing. The deity does not represent any sectarian dogma to the Bhakta but only a common object of universal love or a common spiritual focus. Poetry is another expression of the same fellowship.

Saints also advised for environment protection which indicates their vision. Their literature depicts balance between nature and environment. Saints were rationalist and therefore they accepted all positive thoughts from history and proved that role of saints is not destruction but construction. Saint is not merely a person but it is a tendency, power to live. Saints provide us guided path. Those who follow this path by observing ethics of saints, thoughts of saints reach salvation.

Science and technology has revolutionised human life. But the problems, sorrows continue to exist. Standard of living is lifted but not quality of life. Balance in life is disturbed. Humanity got deteriorated due to money. Man may visit space, but he has hardly any time to look within. The saints are power houses who balance our mind.

Saints are Divine Messengers. It is impossible to weigh the deep debt of gratitude we owe to these divine messengers who bring balance and sanity to a world which gets into pitiful imbalance every now and then. Whenever true knowledge, spiritual knowledge begins to vanish from the face of the earth and tends to lapse into oblivion, the Divine Messengers revive that knowledge and nourish it with the vitality of their own inner experience.

Swami Chidananda in one of his discourses has said "We must always remember Saints. Even for a short moment if we think about the saints, at once we are filled with inspiration and we feel elevated because in their life there is a peculiar power. Due to their humility, they have emptied themselves, so the divine spirit entered in them. They carry a great force and by merely remembering them, we get inner strength and many of our problems are solved. The utterances of saints are not merely to be studied but also to be practiced. Even if we try to put into practice one or two lines of their teachings that will take us to the supreme heights of realisation."

Their metal was recognised all over the world. Saints as a natural genius are known for their achievements, rediscovery, self learning and unconventional ideas equally important to become an effective and successful teacher. Saints always preached and practiced spiritual life.

According to them- spiritual life has not only relevance, it is not only necessary, but it is absolutely indispensable and it is the very central meaning of human life. Spiritual life is the one and only solution of all mankind's unsolved problems and certain fundamental problems such as the problem of old age, disease, death, pain and suffering, the problem of sorrows of human life etc.

Spirituality gives you strength; that inner strength to manage difficult situations and to keep you ever smiling.

Maharashtra has been the land of saints. They purified land and minds of people of Maharashtra through social obligations and betterment of world. They brought progress on spiritual front. We have four Vedas namely Rig Veda, Yajur Veda, Sam Veda and Atharv Veda. The literature of saints is treated as the fifth Veda in Maharashtra.

We cannot gauge the importance of work of Maharashtrian Saints by using scale of twenty first century. We must take into account their "time." The period between 12th and 17th century was the era of famous saints, like Dnyaneshwar, Tukaram, Eknath, Namdeo, Samartha Ramdas, and, Meerabi, Kabir. They were responsible for cultural, spiritual, social development of common man.

Gurudev Ranade describes the saints as-
- **Saint Dnyanaeshwar**- Intellectual Mystic
- **Saint Tukaram**- Personal Mystic
- **Saint Ramdas**- Active Mystic

While as Dr. Mukund Datar suggests-
- **Shri Dnyanesh**- Head of liberated Marathi Culture, Spokesperson of Chidvilas, Chakravarti, Samrat of Saints
- **Shri Tukaram**- Teller of Jeevan Veda, Jagat Guru, Head of universal, practical Bhagwat Dharma
- **Shri Samarth**- Leading the process of converting Nara into Narayana.

These saints showed common people easy path to reach God, which is called Bhaktiyog. That path was Namasmaran, which ultimately merges into transcendental meditation! The continuous 'Namasmaran' leads you to the state of pure consciousness. The 'Nama' melts into your soul gradually and your mind becomes thoughtless. The regular practice of 'Namasmaran' prepares your mind to overcome the difficult situations, in your life and gives you courage and peace of mind which is the true aim of our life. That is 'Moksha' – salvation from worldly pains.

For the attainment of this kind of salvation, you need not get rid of your five senses; because the body and the mind go hand in hand. You are very well supposed to fulfill the wishes of your five senses i.e. to see, listen, smell, test, and touch. You need not lead a life of an ascetic. Saints love peace of mind. They chase truth and immortal happiness in life. They can very well differentiate between truth and untruth. Along with devotion to God, Saints have affection towards society. It is their topic of interest.

CHAPTER 3

Biography of Saint Dnyaneshwar

Sant Dnyāneshwar (1275-1296) was a 13th century Maharashtrian Hindu saint (Sant - a title by which he is often referred), poet, philosopher and yogi of the Nath tradition whose works Bhavartha Deepika (a commentary on Bhagvad Gita, popularly known as "Dnyaneshwari"), and Amrutanubhav are considered to be milestones in Marathi literature.

Dnyaneshwari is the most revered book of the "Warkari" Sect. Every member of that sect regards that book as the base of the "Warkari "sect; but it is a great pity that fully authentic account of the life of the writer of Dnyaneshwari is not known. A few fragments of his life are available in ' Dnyaneshawar Vijay ' by Satchita-nand Baba and a few Abhangas composed by Namdeo. The complete life account of Dnyaneshwar is more or less legendary and has got to be constructed from the fragments of facts selected from the aforesaid books.

Sant Dnyaneshwar was the second of the four children of Vitthal Govind Kulkarni and Rukmini, a pious couple from Apegaon near Paithan on the banks of the river Godavari. Vitthal had studied Vedas and set out on pilgrimages at a young age. In Alandi, about 30 km from Pune, Sidhopant, a local Yajurveda brahmin, was very much impressed with him and Vitthal married his daughter Rukmini. After some time, on getting permission from Rukmini, Vitthal went to

Kashi(Varanasi in Uttar Pradesh, India), where he met Ramananda Swami and requested him to initiate into sannyas, lying about his marriage. But Ramananda Swami later went to Alandi and, came to know that his student Vitthal was the husband of Rukmini, he returned to Kashi and ordered Vitthal to return home to his family. The couple was excommunicated from the brahmin caste as Vitthal had broken with sannyas, the last of the four ashrams. Four children were born to them; Nivrutti in 1273, Dnyandev (Dnyaneshwar) in 1275, Sopan in 1277 and daughter Mukta in 1279. According to some scholars their birth years are 1268, 1271, 1274, and 1277 respectively.

Vitthalpant was already a pious person conversant with the traditions of Indian Philosophy. He was more or less averse to worldly life. He, therefore, appears to have named his children according to the maxims of the Indian philosophy. When one gets out of this worldly life (Nivritti) he obtains real knowledge (Dynana), when real knowledge is obtained, he finds the bridge (Sopan) leading to the liberation or Mukti (Muktabai). These steps of obtaining Moksha (salvation) were as if suggested by Vithalpant by the names of his children.

The couple set out on a pilgrimage with their children to Tryambakeshwar, near Nashik, where their elder son Nivrutti (at the age of 10) was initiated in to the Nath tradition by

Gahininath. The paternal great grandfather of Dnyaneshwar had been initiated into the Nath cult by Goraksha Nath (Gorakh Nath). The orphaned children grew up on alms. They approached the Brahmin community of Paithan to accept them but the Brahmins refused. According to the disputed "Shuddhi Patra" the children were purified by the Brahmins on condition of observing celibacy. Their argument with the Brahmins earned the children fame and respect due to their righteousness, virtue, intelligence, knowledge and politeness. Dnyaneshwar became the student of Nivruttinath along with his younger siblings Sopan and Mukta at the age of 8. He learnt and mastered the philosophy and various techniques of kundalini yoga.

It is believed that later Vitthal and Rukmini ended their lives by jumping into the waters at Prayag where the river Ganges meets Yamuna hoping that their children would be accepted into the society after their death.

Writing

The children moved to Nevasa, a village in Ahmednagar district, where Dnyaneshwar began his literary work when Nivruttinath instructed him to write a commentary on Bhagvad Gita. The Dnyaneshwari or Bhavartha Deepika was written down by Sacchidananandbaba from discourses by Dnyaneshwar. By the time the commentary was complete, Dnyaneshwar was only 15 years old.

Considered a master piece of Marathi literature, the Dnyaneshwari's 18 chapters are composed in a metre called "Ovi". Dnyaneshwar liberated the "divine knowledge" locked in the Sanskrit language to bring that knowledge into Prakrit (Marathi) and made it available to the common man. He was confident that he would write in Marathi in as good or better manner than Sanskrit.

Amrutanubhav, written some time after, is difficult to understand and finds fewer readers. Containing 10 chapters and 806 ovi, the basis of this book is non dualism (advaita siddhanta). The seventh and biggest chapter (295 ovi) is the most important. Apart from Dnyaneshwari and Amrutanubhav works like Changdev Paasashti (a collection of 65 ovi addressed to an allegedly 1400 years old yogi named Changdev Maharaj), Haripath and around 1000 "abhanga" (authorship of many is disputed due to differences in writing style) are attributed to Dnyaneshwar.

Dnyaneshwari (Bhavartha Deepika)

From the internal evidence in Dnyaneshwari, it is clear that this unique criticism on Bhagvad Gita was completed in Shaka 1212. It will be seen from the life of Dnyaneshwar that he composed this book at a very early age of sixteen. The knowledge of all the philosophical books, which were then in existence, the different theories of life, the knowledge of the customs and manners of the people of his times and all such things which are evident from the book, simply make the readers wonder how a boy of sixteen could acquire so much maturity and knowledge at that age; but as Lord Krishna has himself expressed in Bhagvad Gita " a very learned person takes rebirth in a great family with all his achievements" and hence he proves to be a prodigy. Hence as believers in rebirth, we might say that the knowledge already acquired by Dnyaneshwar in the previous birth came along with him in his present birth. Though Dnyaneshwari is apparently a criticism on the Bhagvad Gita, still we find that it is really an independent book expounding the Indian Philosophy. It has only taken Bhagvad Gita as its base, because it was a known book revered by all. The very fact that the commentary on 700 and odd shloks of Bhagvad Gita should expand into over 8,500 ' ovis goes to prove the independent nature of the book.

Dnyaneshwari is not important only from the point of view of philosophy; it also is a very good example of poetry full of imagination. The use of language is also unique. The words and phrases used are so very appropriate that nobody has been able to suggest so far a substitute for any one of them. The figures of speech like simile, metaphor etc. is met with very often in the book. They are not only appropriate but they show profuse knowledge on the part of the author. The language used is so captivating that any reader will agree to the statement made by Dnyaneshwar that he will get a certificate from his appreciative readers that the Marathi language is even sweeter than the nectar.

Dnyaneshwar was a Yogi. He appeared to be well-versed in all practices of Yoga. Whenever he spoke of Yoga and its practices he appeared to be speaking with so much confidence that we feel that he is speaking not from hear say but from his personal experience. The ultimate live Samadhi (Sanjeevan Samadhi), that Dnyaneshwar took, to put an end to his life, shows also that he had full knowledge of the practice of Yoga. Along with Yoga, Dnyaneshwar has not neglected other ways of devotion like "Bhakti" and worship of the idol of the God. He has done enough justice to all these whenever necessary and has also described their importance in human life.

In Fifteen Hundred Six, Saint Eknath, disciple of Saint Dnyanaeshwar most reverentially refined the quality of Dnyanaeshwari. Indeed the scripture was originally genuine and immaculate for certain; however, it had been adulterated due to wrong memorisation and recitations in the meantime. The present version of Dnyaneshwari is immaculate and sacred.

Other Literary Work

Even though, as pointed out before, Dnyaneshwari is as good as an independent work, though technically speaking it is a commentary on Bhagwatgeeta, the story goes that, when after completing Dnyaneshwari, Dnyaneshwar went to Nivrittinath, whom he called his Guru, he said, "This is after all a commentary. It is not an independent work. So I want you to do some independent work." Hence Dnyaneshwar wrote the "Amritanubhava" or "Anubhava-mrit "in which he has stated his experiences in Yoga and Philosophy, whereby we can get the experience of nectar. This work of Dnyaneshwar, though not so much universally acknowledged, is also as great and important as Dnyaneshwari itself. The style of writing, the use of words and phrases the use of figures of speech, the ease in writing and the confidence with which the book is written leave no doubt that the work must be of the Dnyaneshwar himself. The subject of this book is abstract and is dealt with great brevity and directness.

One more book in Ovi form under the caption of "Yoga Vashishtha" goes as a work of Dnyaneshwar; but on close study of the book, though it appears to be written in the same style as that of Dnyaneshwari, it is felt that the grace of the words and the poetic imagination is not of the same level as that in Dnyaneshwari. The scholars of Marathi literature have therefore a serious doubt whether this work is of the same Dnyaneshwar who composed Dnyaneshwari. It is suspected that somebody else has imitated the style of

Dnyaneshwari and has pawned his own work under the name of Dnyaneshwar.

Apart from the above works there are about 1200 Abhangas said to be composed by Dnyaneshwar, but on their close examination it is found that all of them are not of the same standard. From the style of the use of words, the ideas and the philosophy embodied therein it can be said that only about two to three hundred of these abhangas must have been composed by Dnyaneshwar and the others are composed and interspersed by other writers.

Varkari Movement

"DNYANDEVE RACHILA PAYA, TUKA ZALASI KALAS". (Dnyaneshwar Maharaj built/ started Bhakti movement temple in Maharashtra and Tukaram Maharaj became the crown.) Dnyaneshwar introduced the Varkari Movement (or Vitthala Sampradaya) of Pandharpur (founder of the Varkari movement). The Varkaris consider him as their teacher and spiritual leader, who initiated his contemporaries associated with the Dvaita (dualism) school of the bhakti movement into Advaita (non-dualism). He strongly advocated Dnyana yukta bhakti (devotion guided by knowledge). In the limited field of spiritualism, he destroyed strong societal frame work and created a feeling amongst all fractions of society that at least for God, we all are his children. This is revolutionary work.

The philosophy was complicated and difficult to understand, but he simplified it for the benefit of common man.

Entering into a State of Samadhi

After composing 'Amritanubhava', Dnyaneshwar went to visit the holy places along with Namdeo and other saints of his time. In his Abhangas known as "Tirthawali " Namdeo has given a graphic description of this their visit to the holy places from which we know that Dnyaneshwar had visited many holy places of his day.

After completing their visits to the holy places, Dnyaneshwar felt that the mission of his life was over. He therefore, expressed his intention to take live Samadhi. On the 13th day of the second half of Kartik in Shaka 1218 Dnyaneshwar took live Samadhi at Alandi. An account of this heartrending incident is graphically pictured by Namdeo in his Abhangas known as "Samadheeche Abhanga ".After the departure of Dnyaneshwar, the brothers also therefore decided to end their existence in this world and within a year's time from the Samadhi of Dnyaneshwar they all left this perishable world.

Pasayadan

Dnyaneshwar wrote the Pasayadan which is a prayer for the general well being of the people. Pasaydan is included at the end of the Dynaneshwari.. Mauli (affectionate mother) Dnyaneshwar maharaj completed his work on Shrimat

Bhagvad Gita (Having 700 Vowels in 18 chapters) called as Gyaneshwari or Dnyaneshwari which has 9000 vowels. Pasayadan is a 9 vowels work written at end of Dnyaneshwari's 18th Chapter. This Pasayadan describe Message of these 9000 vowels.

CHAPTER 4

Biography of Saint Tukaram

Saint Tukaram (1609-1650) was one of the greatest poet saints ever born in India. According to Sir Alexander Grant (1826-1884) Tukaram is a National Poet. He is quite renowned for his contribution to Bhakti Movement of Maharashtra. The exact records related to the life history of Tukaram are not available. So, there is a little disagreement regarding his exact birth date. It is considered to be one of the four - 1568 AD, 1577 AD, 1609 AD or 1598 AD. Tukaram vanished without a trace in 1650. What little we know of his life is a reconstruction from his own autobiographical poems, the contemporary poetess Bahinabai's memoirs in verse, and the latest biographer of Marathi poet-saints, Mahipati's account. The rest is all folklore, though it cannot be dismissed on those grounds alone. Modern scholars such as late V.S. Bendre have made arduous efforts to collate evidences from disparate contemporary sources to establish a well-researched biography of Tukaram. But even this is largely conjectural.

Bolhoba had three sons: Savji was the eldest, followed by Tukaram and Kanhoba, the youngest. The family in which Tukaram was born was indeed a very pious one. The family was also very cultured and religious. Worship of Lord Vithoba had been its hallmark for generations together and so was the annual pilgrimage to Pandharpur. The family also had the distinction of being Mahajans (money-lenders). It owned farmland engaged in money-lending and trade. The family owned two wadas (houses) at Dehu: one for residence and the other, in the marketplace, for trade and business. It enjoyed the respect of the villagers and also of those living in the immediate environs. They were called kunbis (farming community), because they engaged in agriculture and vanis (trading community) because of trading. However, Tukaram abjured all these, because of which he was called as gosavi (someone like a fakir). Nevertheless, 'Gosavi' was never the surname of the family. It was 'More' and 'Gosavi' was an honorific.

Tukaram was only seventeen when his father and spiritual mentor, Bolhoba, passed away. No sooner had he managed to overcome this grief then his mother, Kanakai, departed from the world the very next year.

Tukaram was just twenty-one when the whole region found itself in the grip of an unprecedented famine. There was belated rainfall in 1629 and ultimately, crops were lost due to a surfeit of rain. However, people still held on to their hopes. The next year, 1630, was one of drought. Now people became desperate. The prices of essential commodities went up sky-high. Cattle perished by the hundred in the absence of feed and many people died of sheer starvation. Even well-to-do families became impoverished. The cup of people's woes began overflowing,

The next year (1631), this marked the culmination of natural calamity. It was a year of tremendously excessive rainfall, because of which all crops were washed away. Life everywhere was thrown into disarray. The family of Tukaram suffered very much in this time of great adversity. He lost all his cattle. The money-lending business was lost. Tukaram's first wife, Rakhumabai, and his beloved, only son, Santoba, fell prey to the famine.

He faced them all, did not run away from them. He never was an escapist. He was desirous of conquest in the work-a-day life and also wanted to cull the elixir of it all. All these disasters had made him evaluate money, the human situation and human relationships. The futility of it all had amply been borne in upon him. His quest now was directed towards the permanent values. He began thinking in terms of sailing through all these to reach the shore yonder. He set out for the Bhandara Mountain in search of truth. No coming back till he found the immortal truth. That was his determination. Wild animals attacked him and reptiles troubled him, but Tukaram remained undeterred. His perseverance reached fruition on the fifteenth day when he encountered Eternal Truth. Now instead of attending to his worldly affairs, Tukaram decided to renovate the temple that had suffered the ravages of famine, thus proclaiming to the world that he had now definitely taken the metaphysical path.

He perused in right earnest the Dnyanaeshwari and Amrutanubhav of Dnyaneshwar, Eknath's criticism of the Bhagawat, Bhavartha Ramayan, Swatmanubhav and the religious compositions of Namdev and Kabir. He memorised the sayings of all these great saints.

Tukaram partook of this saintly offering, which had given a figure and form to the Eternal Principle essentially devoid of both. He also had recourse to the ancient Puranas and ancient sciences.

Verses (abhang) began gushing forth from his mouth and the fortunate among the people began listening to him. His abhangs encapsulated the essence of ancient shrutis and shastras in a very lucid manner. Tukaram used to do kirtan at the gate of Dnyaneshwar's abode at Alandi.

The great scholar Rameshwar Bhat happened to listen to those sweet compositions. He was surprised to find the essence of the Bhagvad-Gita and the Eknathi Bhagawat in the Prakrit language and with such lucidity! He was scandalised and denounced this novel happening. He said,

'Your abhangs elucidate the essence of the Vedas, which is not your right. It is sacrilegious to listen to it from your mouth. Who incited you to undertake such an enterprise?' Tukaram said, 'It is not my own speech, it is God speaking through me.'

Tukaram now began delivering his discourses and kirtan with renewed vigour, for it was the means chosen by him for people's edification and uplift. Tukaram disappeared at the age of forty-one. Varkaris believe that Vitthal Himself carried Tukaram away to heaven in a "chariot of light".

"Tukaram was arguably the greatest poet in Marathi Langugage. Tukaram's genius partly lies in his ability to transform the external world into its spiritual analogue. Tukaram's stature in Marathi literature is comparable to that of Shakespeare in English or Goethe in German. He could be called the quintessential Marathi poet reflecting the genius or the language as well as its characteristics literary culture. There is no other Marathi writer who has so deeply and widely influenced Marathi Literary Culture since. Poetry as a genre is incomplete without Tukaram. Tukaram may have written his poems in loneliness but he recited them to live audiences in a shrine of Vitthal. Hundreds of people gathered to listen to his poetry. The poetess Bahinabai, a contemporary and a devoted follower of Tukaram has described how Tukaram in a state of trance, chanted his poems while an enraptured audience rocked to their rhythm. This has been a tradition from the time of Dnyaneshwar (1275-1296), the founder of Marathi poetry and the cult of

Vithoba and Namdeo (1270-1350), the great forerunner of Tukaram. The audience consisted of common village-folk, including women and low-caste people, thrilled by the heights their own language scaled and stirred by the depths it touched.

Religion in Maharashtra, in Tukaram's time, was a practice that separated communities, classes and castes. Bhakti was the middle way between the extremes of Brahminism on the one hand and folk religion on the other. It was also the most democratic and egalitarian community of worshippers, sharing a way of life and caring for all life with a deep sense of compassion. The legacy of Jainism and Buddhism had not disappeared altogether in Maharashtra. It was regenerated in the form of Bhakti. Tukaram's penetrating criticism of the degenerated state of Brahminical Hinduism and his scathing comments on bigotry and obscurantism profiteering and profligacy in the name of religion, bear witness to his universal humanistic concerns. He had the abhorrence of a true realist for any superstitious belief or practice. He understood the nature of language well enough to understand how it can be used to bewitch, mislead and distort. He had a healthy suspicion of god-men and gurus. He believed that the individual alone was ultimately responsible for his own spiritual liberation. He was not an escapist. His mysticism was not rooted in a rejection of reality but rather in a spirited response to it after its total acceptance as a basic fact of life. Tukaram's hard common sense is not contracted by his mysticism: the two reinforce each other.

Some people believe that Tukaram just vanished into thin air while singing his poetry in front of an ecstatic audience on the bank of the river Indrayani in Dehu. Some others speculate that he was murdered by his enemies. Still others think that he ended his own life by drowning himself into the very river where his poems had been sunk earlier.

Reading his farewell poems, however, one is inclined to imagine that Tukaram bade a proper farewell to his close friends and fellow-devotees and left his native village for some unknown destination with no intention of returning. He asked them to return home after their having walked a certain distance with him. He told them that they would never see him again as he was "going home for good". He told them that from then on only "talk about Tuka" would remain in "this world".

Some of the teachings of Saint Tukaram are listed below-

1. An individual should make God the center of his universe. Serving others and loving others is the best way through which we can find Him.
2. For the attainment of sadhana, an individual needs to have faith in his/her destiny.

3. It is not necessary to renounce the world and lead the life of an ascetic in order to be one with God. Spirituality does not require elaborate rituals.
4. Nama Japa (reciting the name of Lord) is the most important privilege of being a devotee.
5. Siddhis serve as impediments in the attainment of genuine sadhana (meditation).
6. Traditions prevent an individual from budding in the love of God. One has to sidestep the usual customs to achieve the same.

CHAPTER 5
Biography of Samarth Ramdas Swami

In Maharashtra, the period between 12th and 17th century was the era of the famous saints, like Dnyaneshwar, Tukaram, Eknath, Namdeo, Samartha Ramdas, and, Meerabi, Kabir etc. in North India.

Samartha Ramdas (1608-1682) has written approximately 40,000 verses, a verse of four lines each, in different books. His life can be described in four distinct milestones-

- 1608 to1620- Childhood
- 1620 to 1632- Period of Penance
- 1632 to 1644- Travelling
- 1644 to1678- Community awakening

Early Days

Ramdas was born in 1608, in the Shak year 1530 on the occasion of 9th day of the bright fortnight of Chaitra, the first month of the year. His native place was a small village by name Jaamb, in Aurangabad District. His father, Suryajipant Thosar and mother was Ranubai. Ramdas was given the name as Narayana. The family belonged to Brahmin community. The family had devotion of Lord Ramachandra going on for many generations and it was a custom to celebrate the birth anniversary of Lord Ramachandra, which was the date on which Narayana was also born. The childhood of Narayana is punctuated by various strange and miraculous happenings.

Gangadhar, his elder brother was a religious-minded, peaceful, obedient son, while Narayana was inquisitive in nature, had adventurous spirit, very strong in body and mind and he was always playing wild games, swimming, roaming in deep jungles and sometimes going to a secluded place and meditating for hours. His entire behaviour was extraordinary. His father was authority on spiritual matters and when elder brother was given initiation, Narayana also insisted for it but it was refused.

After some days, when he was about 12 years old his mother insisted that Narayana should get married. Despite his resistance, mother somehow prevailed. When he was standing on "Bohala" for wedding, it so happened that while the priests were reciting the blessings with the last words as Savadhan (attention! be alert!!), Narayana in the quest of his spiritual life ran away from the ceremony. He went to Nasik, on the banks of Godavari and at a quiet place called Takli, he stayed alone, with an intention to do penance for blessings of Lord Ramachandra. As a devotion to Sun God, he started Gayatri Mantra Anushthan. He recited Mantra for hours together, by standing waist deep in the stream of the river. For twelve years he lived there doing penance. By that time he became well known in the surrounding areas as a pure seeker of very high order. He was a young man of 24, with perfect athletic body and the Mastery over occult powers.

Travelling

Now with a desire to witness the condition of his country and countrymen, Ramdas set about on a journey throughout the country. This had two objectives- First was to acquaint himself with the lamentable conditions of Hindu subjects under the reign of Moghuls and to infuse the militant spirit in the Hindus by establishing temples of Hanuman at as many places as possible. These temples were the centers of physical training and religious revival among Hindus. There was thus a large network of monasteries called 'MATH". They were not only centers of activities but also a source of communication in the days of war. Ramdas also visited Saint Tukaram of Dehu. By his efforts, there was tremendous awakening in the community in Maharashtra.

It is recorded in history, that it was Kalyan who wrote down the manuscripts of Dasbodh, as dictated by Ramdas in a cave near Shivthar, a hilly village near Mahad, in Raigad District.

Ramdas' Time

"This was 17th century Maharashtra. In those days, several autocratic and unjust rulers ruled medieval India. The local political elite kowtowed with the invaders, who came lured by the wealth and vast tracts of fertile land. As these invaders usurped power, the elite became their local partners. Also in the absence of any state support, droughts and floods caused tremendous strain on the population. People were burdened under heavy discriminatory taxes like Jiziya, and had to fork out huge sums to pay to the callous administration. Thus they were economically exploited and little was left for them to support their lives. Common people were subjected to the loot and the plunder at the hands of the rulers' mercenary forces and the members of the administration. Women were abducted and raped. There was widespread dissatisfaction and disillusionment about the rulers, but in the absence of organised resistance, people had no choice but to suffer. They had lost confidence in themselves and preferred to remain sufferers. In utter desperation, the society leaned towards religious rituals, ignoring the core spiritual wisdom".

Shankar Abhyankar in his book on "Ramdas" maintains that all saints of Maharashtra tried to improve the moral standards of the society which was devastated by external raids. But, only Ramdas, while fully deciphering the raider's nefarious designs, had taken them head on. In fact he is the only saint who has been referred as 'Samarth". (Capable, Competent). He has never abused woman in his writings. Samarth is a unique saint, who had no formal Guru.

Human development comes to a standstill if there is no political freedom and social justice. Able leadership is an essential ingredient for any desirable change. When most of the social actors are depressed and disorganised, a leader has to show the path. Anarchy like situation warrants the leadership to first change the mindset of people. Throughout world history, physical change has followed an ideological one. Organisational change has to be supported by changing in thinking from those who govern the organisational systems. Samarth Ramdas along with Saint Tukaram and Sant Dnyaneshwar collectively contributed to the change in the minds of Maharashtrians. Thus these saints are in true sense "CHANGE AGENTS."

WRITINGS OF SAMARTH RAMDAS SWAMI

Karunshtake

Ramdas left home when he was only twelve years old. Although he had strong control over his emotions, it was not easy to lead lonesome and hard life, during his self-training period.

In that restless state of mind, Ramdas wrote Karunashtake. These are the prayers full of pathos or "Karuna rasa". So these are called Karunshtake.

Manache Shlok

His "Manache Shlok" (verses addressed to mind) is meant for seekers of truth, are very popular in these modern days. These 205 Shlokas are recited by heart in many schools and are heavily commented upon by eminent scholars. 'Manache Shlok or Manobodh' includes 205 shlok with four lines each. Since the 17th century, 'Manache Shlok is being recited by common people in Maharashtra. Many have learnt them by heart, since the style of shloks is unique, easy, beautiful and simple, though artistic and meaningful.

Samarth Ramdas teaches us to have dialogue with our own mind. Your own mind is your friend, your enemy and your own mind can be also your Guru.

205 verses of Manache Shlok are translated into several Indian languages, including Urdu. A Muslim Saint Shahsuraj Ali has translated it into Urdu, which is called "Manasamazavana ". His Guru was Ramdas. The handwritten copy of "Manasamzavana "still exists in the Jama Masjid of Delhi.

Atmaram, Karunatake, Abhanga and Arti are his other books. All popular Marathi Artis e.g. 'Sukhakarta Dukhhartha, Durge durghata bhari, Shivaarti, Maruti Stotra and many others are written by Ramdas.

Ramdas thought, the best guide to advise the human being is his own mind. Manache Shlok teaches your mind to change yourself gradually. Find out the reasons of your anger, jealousy, greed, sorrow, depression, fear, because these are the negative emotions, which you have to face constantly in your life.

Dasbodh

Dasbodh is the most important book by Ramdas. The book consists of 7,751 verses. "Das" means servant i.e. a devotee. Ramdas was a devotee of Ram. "Bodh" means "teaching".

In 'Dasbodh', Ramdas touches multiple topics connected to human life. The book is a beautiful guide for the ideal human life. It teaches us how to shape our life through Ramdas' excellent practical and spiritual principles.

Dasbodh also explains multiple facets of the Universe. It really covers the whole cosmos. Ramdas, however, emphasises the existence of God very strongly and shows common people the easy way to reach God, namely, 'Bhaktimarg'. This, according to him, is a sure path to achieve
Peace of mind in life.
Samarth realised that the base of a firm and healthy society is a harmonious family. One should not neglect his family. He should fulfil his duties first; otherwise, he is not fit for devoting himself to God.
Samarth handles in "Dasbodh" varied themes, for example, family planning, health, body facts, architecture, construction of buildings, administration, politics, time management, personal development, how to train managers and leaders, management of your own mind and spiritual thoughts. After Veda Vyasa, only Samarth has touched upon so many subjects in one book. From first step of Prapancha (Domestic Life) to the last step of Nivrutti (Spiritual retired life), he has dealt with everything. It took 48 years for Samarth to complete this book, for a very simple reason that he followed "Walk the Talk" principle while writing this book.

Great people like Gandhi, and Vivekananda had read Dasbodh and had written words of praise on "Dasbodh".

Dasbodh is the main literary work of Ramdas and in addition to that he has composed prodigious poetry on various subjects in various meters. Many poems are dedicated to give practical instructions as well as spiritual advice. The poetry runs into volumes and consists of such varieties like Abhangas, Ovis, Sawai, Phatka, (traditional folk medium for communication) Hymns, Aarti, Shlokas, and occasional descriptions of ceremonies, materials used for buildings, arrangements to be made for big functions etc. One gets a pleasant surprise to find an unexpected minute observations, or work of epic size on Ramayana. He stands apart from other saint poets, by his freedom of choice of other subjects than the devotional and philosophical sermonising. The main purpose behind his writings was to awaken the worldly wise or lazy people to the need of devotion. The mission of Ramdas was quite unique unlike other saints, because he was greatly involved in political affairs for uplifting Hindus against the rulers. He chose language which common people can understand and also chose media for his expression which are close to hearts of common people.

Atmaram

Samarth Ramdas noticed that in spite of listening, reading and meditation, the desired expected change in the attitude of human beings was not witnessed; therefore, he guides them through the medium of conversation.

In "Atmaram", Ramdas has presented a transparent fundamental thought. Samarth has guided his disciples through "Atmaram", to practice their search for self realisation. The verses in Atmaram are purely philosophical. "Atma" means soul, "Ram" means here "Supreme Being." The idea is: an individual soul of each and every being in the universe is a part of the "Supreme Being".

Atmaram consists of 183 verses. These verses are like deep Spiritual Ocean, wherein you learn to dive and find out shells full of radiant pearls.

In this era scientists have successfully tried to explore space. Samarth Ramdas advises through his valuable work, to find out the space in your deep inner mind. He wants you to design your life more beautifully in an artistic way, filling it with pure happiness and peace!

"To know yourself, to find out your hidden self is knowledge"

Later years of his life

In about 1655 A.D. he visited Tanjore in South India and met Vyankoji- brother of Shivaji. During these days, Ramdas gave initiations to thousands of deserving persons. Ramdas kept himself abreast with each and every happening in the country.

In 1682, on the 9th day of dark fortnight of Magha Month of Shaka 1603 Ramdas felt that the last day of his life had come. At the hour of 12 noon, his spirit left his body.

Ramdas lived for 71 years, and except for the 12 years of his childhood, the whole of his life was a long story of great efforts for regeneration of religion, politics, and discipline in devotional matters as well as practical life.

Ramdas was having good knowledge of classical music as well as folk music. We find in him an artist par excellence in description of the beauty of nature or graphic narration of human pathos. He was a keen observer of nature as well as social manners, behaviour of various people, their virtues and vices, their achievements and failures and the life of poverty and political plight due to apathy and inaction. He abhorred laziness and always upheld the value of consistent efforts and personal wisdom; He knew Sanskrit and Urdu as well. He was truly a leader of leaders.

He initiated an independent cult, by name "Swa-swaroop Sampradaya" which is a discipline of spiritual instructions. This Sampradaya was popular and is still an active organisation in spiritual life of Maharashtra. His teachings are available in his books and profuse literature produced by many of his disciples. These have touched the heart of aspirants and given them a light of hope and liberation.

Though Ramdas personally liked a life of meditation and seclusion, he put his own liking aside in order to mix with people, educate them and organise them to achieve "Ananda-Vana-Bhuvan" a society and a place where everybody is happy. All people are indebted to him for his inspiring messages.

He was tremendously active in all walks of life. Perhaps no other saint of his time had taken so deep interest in the comprehensive upliftment of people for which his Swaroop-Sampradaya is very ardently making all efforts even in these modern days with its great emphasis on discipline, diligence, devotion and study, regularity of daily practice and collective participation in various organisational activities under the guidance of Mahantas appointed in various Maths.

Samarth Ramdas's work is comparable with Hegel, Joseph Mazzini and Saint Loyola of Italy.

Samarth Ramdas is ever living in the memory of all devotees as well as workers in socio-political field and his Dasbodh is always a source of inspiration to all towards a better individual and collective life culminating in happiness for all.

CHAPTER 6

Shrimat Bhagvad Gita

According to Hindu belief, Shrimat Bhagvad Gita is the ultimate statement of spiritual knowledge since it was professed by Lord Krishna who was an avatar of the supreme God. The Bhagvad Gita is one phase of the Tripod of Indian philosophy and culture, the other two phases being the Upanishads and the Brahmasutra. While the Upanishads lay the foundation of the loftiest reach possible for humanity and the Brahmasutras logically elucidate the intricate issues involved in the Upanishads, the Bhagvad Gita blends together the Transcendent and the Immanent features of the Ultimate reality, bringing together into an integrated whole knowledge and action, the inner and the outer, the individual and the society, man and God, all which are portrayed as facets of a Universal Operation, presenting entire life and all life as a perfectly complete organic wholeness. To teach how the Upanishads can actually be practiced, how they can be made basis of our daily life is the purpose of Gita. Leaving nothing unsaid and attempting to solve every problem of life. It is said, once you get knowledge of yourself by understanding Gita, you can overcome dejection, despair, hopelessness and a total breakdown of self-confidence. This is because, the Gita starts in defeatism and ends in victory. The final verse affirms victory and fulfillment.

The Bhagvad Gita is considered a holy text of verses, which holds the answers to some of the most perplexing philosophical, theological, and spiritual questions of life. It contains suitable practical examples to tackle situations in which a person feels that he is battling for freedom from all the materialistic things in life. But it is not just a declaration of experienced truth. It is not merely an expounding of a certain revelation. But from start to finish, it is dialectic in its method of approaching situations in life, various problems and conflicts that surround a person as we try to execute the journey. Philosophy of Gita is an educative process of bringing the individual from a state of wrong understanding, a state of mixed-up interior, a state of confusion into a higher state of right understanding, clarity of perception and vision and a very clear interior.

Bhagvad Gita preaches about believing in the existence of a supreme being and acquiring the ability to differentiate between good and evil. Even after so many centuries of its creation, this book is still regarded as the most sacred text of Hinduism.

Bhagvad Gita has been acclaimed to be a gospel of life. It is philosophy of life. In Dnyanaeshwari, saint Dnyanaeshwar has described Gita as **"Philosophical Science."** The importance of Bhagvad Gita is in its offering satisfactory solutions to the problems that beset mankind of all times.

Gandhi had said "Whenever I am in trouble, and find darkness around me, I turn to Gita. I get instant pleasure."

Huxley says, "Gita is gist of permanent philosophy which is very simple and straight forward. It is for entire mankind."

Karl Steen Hunser from Germany said, "Gita would be Bible for all the nations of the world. I am still more wondering why there are so many religions in the world."

Swami Sivananda is one of the great exponents of the philosophy, religion and the technique of the Bhagvad Gita system, and his commentary is regarded as one of the most authoritative expositions available. While describing glory of Gita, Swami Sivananda says "it is a dialogue between Lord Krishna and Arjuna, narrated in Bhishma- Parva of Mahabharata." According to Yogi Arbindo "It is a pair of Divine Teacher and Human Disciple." It comprises 18 chapters of a total of 700 Sanskrit verses. Considerable matter has been condensed and compressed in these verses. In the whole world-literature there is no book so elevating and so inspiring as the Gita. The Gita expounds very lucidly the cardinal principles or the fundamentals of the Hindu Dharma. It is the source of all the wisdom. Gita is the cream of the Vedas. It is the essence of the Upanishads. It is the universal scripture for all the people of all temperaments and for all times. Gita has sublime thoughts and practical instructions on Yoga, devotion, Vedanta and action. The Gita is a unique book for all ages. It is a book that comes under the category of Prasthanatraya. It deals with the four Yogas- Karma Yoga, Bhakti Yoga, Raj Yoga and Dnyana Yoga.

The teachings of Gita are broad, universal and sublime. They do not belong to any cult, sect, creed, particular age, place or country. They are meant for the people of the entire world at large. It has a message for the solace, peace, freedom, salvation and perfection of all human beings.

The whole world is battle field. The real kurukshetra is within you. The battle of Mahabharata is still raging within you. Ignorance (Avidya) is Dhritarashtra. The individual soul is Arjuna. The Indweller who dwells in your heart is Lord Krishna, the charioteer. The body is your chariot. The senses (Indriyas) are the horses. The mind, egoism, senses, Samskaras (mental impressions), Vasanas (latent tendencies), cravings, Raga-Dvesha (likes and dislikes), lust, jealousy, greed, pride and hypocrisy are your dire enemies.

Man is a composite of three fundamental factors, viz. cognition, feeling and will. There are people with three kinds of temperaments – the active, the emotional and the rational.

So there are the three Yogas- Dnyana Yoga (or men of enquiry and self- analysis), Bhakti Yoga (for men of emotional temperament) and Karma Yoga for the man of active temperament. Any Yoga amongst these three is as efficacious as the other.

Gita proposes the theory of the three Margas (paths) - the Dnyana Marga, the Bhakti Marga, and the Karma Marga. There is no conflict between them; on the contrary Gita harmonises the philosophy of action, devotion and knowledge. The three horses of this body- chariot- action, emotion and intellect should work in perfect harmony.

The Gita is divided into three sections illustrative of "Tat- Tvam- Asi". According to this view, the first six chapters deal with the path of action- Karma Yoga, the next six explain the path of devotion or Bhakti Yoga and the last six treat of the path of knowledge or Dnyana Yoga.

While drawing the essence of the Gita, it is felt that the Gita emphasises again and again that one should cultivate an attitude of detachment. It urges repeatedly that one should live in the world like lotus-leaf, which is unaffected by the surroundings. Thus the eighteenth chapter should be studied again and again. It contains the quintessence of the whole Gita Sastra.

In the book "Hindu Genius is Universal" the author Ravi Kumar quotes **Einstein** as follows;

"We owe a lot of Indians who taught us how to count, without which no worthwhile discovery could have been made. I have made the Gita as the main source of my inspiration and guide for the purpose of scientific investigations of my theories."

Reading Gita has become mandatory even in the US University. The objective is to help college students get a grasp of 'the perennial questions' in their 'journey of transformation'.

Since last year, all students of business management at Seton Hall University (SHU), New Jersey, have had to compulsorily study the Bhagvad Gita. Not to glean some tactical insights for use in corporate warfare, but to ground themselves in multiple religious cultures. A laudable objective that would resonate with US President Barrack Obama's vision of a pluralist America where Christians and Muslims, Hindus and Jews, and non-believers, live together.

It all began as a pilot project last year, to teach the Gita to business students as a 'signature course' on a full-time basis. From this year, the Gita has become part of the core curriculum at the SHU, which happens to be a Roman Catholic-run institution.

Ironically enough, the initiative was triggered by a concern that the proportion of 'active' Catholics filling the faculty and administrative positions was falling. This was making it difficult for the college to maintain its religious identity. The university then constituted a group, and entrusted it with the task of designing an inter-disciplinary course that would help students obtain answers to "perennial questions". Naturally, this being part of an effort to emphasise the university's Roman Catholic identity, the answers were to be sought in the Bible, which would be made compulsory reading.

That's when AD Amar, professor of strategy, policy and knowledge in the university's School of Business stepped in. As a member of the core curriculum group, he suggested that looking for perennial questions in the Bible would not yield insights from different civilisations and that "it would give students only one perspective."

The faculty then asked that the answers to the perennial questions "be expanded". Eventually they decided to consider the 'answers' as given by various religions, including Islam and Buddhism. "Many Americans do not understand Hinduism. They find it too complex. In fact, Americans find Buddhism simple and feel it can be imbibed from one known leader, such as the Dalai Lama."

So at one of the core curriculum meetings, Amar proposed that Hinduism should be included. As the world's oldest religion, he argued, it had put in most thought into the 'perennial questions.' His suggestion was accepted, and the SHU committee included Gita, along with the Koran, the Bible, besides texts from the Buddhist sutras and the Greek philosophers. The course was called The "Journey of Transformation".

"American students will find Gita rather difficult to navigate due to cultural barriers and a lack of context. But they are all fascinated by India, and being keen to learn, they will be interested."

The Journey of Transformation will be taught alongside another course, **"Christianity And Culture In Dialogue"**. The University will train faculty to take these additional courses, and whoever agrees to take it on will get a stipend of $1,000 for training, and a 'bounty' of another $1,000 the first time they teach the course. While six new professors were hired last year for this course, another six are set to be hired this year. If other universities, too, take a leaf out of SHU's book, then America could well churn out a new generation of business graduates well-versed in the perennial questions. If the recession is still on by the time they pass out, a spiritual grounding in the Gita could prove more than useful.[13]

Yogi Arbindo has said "In the Gita there is very little that is merely local or temporal and its spirit is so large, profound and universal that even this little can easily be universalised without the sense of the teaching suffering any diminution or violation; rather by giving an ampler scope to it than belonged to the country and epoch, the teaching gains in depth, truth and power. What is of entirely permanent value is that which besides being universal has been experienced, lived and seen with a higher than the intellectual vision. I hold it; therefore of small importance to extract from Gita its exact metaphysical connotation as it was understood by the men of the time, even if that were accurately possible."

"Shrimat Bhagvad Gita is the path-finder for those struggling in mires of the mundane world with all sorts of pains and pleasures, the duality of happiness and grief, the perennial uncertainties, doubts and the dark clouds of make-belief, moreover lack of Knowledge and wisdom about the Nature of one's own Self !"

Shankaracharya (Shankarbhashya), Saint Dnyanaeshwar (Dnyanaeshwari) and Lokmanya Tilak (Gita-Rahasya) can be treated as representatives of three time spans of different era who have commented on Gita. The difference in interpretation of Gita by these authors is acceptable to Gita according to many seers. This book has ambiguity but it can be taken as plus point since it has attracted people of different traditions across globe.

It is claimed that there are 118 versions of Gita. Even in Dasbodh, Samarth has given a list of seventeen versions of Gita. Abstraction is visible in Upanishadas, Vedas and Gita and they are known as "Prasthantrayi". Gita has both evolutions of Indian Culture as well as progression.

Dr. Kher, Shri Narhar Kurundkar, Dr. Damodar Kosambi, Dr. Sant, Mahatma Gandhi, Yogi Arbiondo and many more have written on Gita. Like human being, Gita Jayanti is celebrated every year, although the exact details of birth of Gita are not available. This only proves that Gita is constantly evolving.

Each evolutionary book has two parts- one is within reach of mind and the other is visionary. Probably because of this reason, Gita is still studied. Gita has drama coupled with philosophy. The third dimension is human relations. Gita being in dialogue form, it brings different shades of relations between Lord Krishna and Arjuna. Gita is in poetry form and not prose. This further reduces the distance between book and the reader.

In fact the occasion to announce supreme wisdom was certainly unusual although most appropriately timed; a great war of gigantic proportion between Pandavas and Kauravas was about to begin!

"The war was indeed symbolic of the battle between right and wrong, truth verses untruth, dharma against adharma. The venue was Kurukshetra (literally meaning- field of action); moreover it was Dharmayuddha (a battle governed and monitored by pre-set rules and regulations)! Here Krishna is Counsellor, Arjuna is Counselee while as Gita is the "session-notes" of the counseling process".

Gita has Dnyana Yoga (Thought Process), Bhakti Yoga (Emotions) and Karma Yoga (Action, Behaviour) - all independent as well as blended together. Gita aims at controlling emotions and orienting Arjuna towards action.

Gita talks about excellence and suggests that we can reach there. It has flexibility as well to accommodate all kinds of people.

Background

The main warrior of the Pandavas- Arjuna, who has his charioteer in Lord Krishna Himself, suddenly becomes sad and despondent on seeing "his very own –Kith and kin, friends and relatives, lined up in the opposite camp for battle; with an extreme sense of dejection, he decided not to go ahead with the battle and lays down his arms. The sense of 'me' and 'myness' suddenly drains out his entire strength and might, out of total dejection. Lord Krishna diagnoses the ailment bothering Arjuna quickly and comes out with the remedy- namely an admonition with simultaneous wise counsel! The Dialogue between the Lord and Arjuna is the celestial song "Bhagvad Gita."

Gita was expounded to Arjuna by none other than Lord Krishna Himself and which is included in the Epic Mahabharata authors by Sage Vyas Mahamuni. This 18 chaptered bunch of verses extols the Nectarine "Advaita" (Non-dualism) philosophy and exhorts everyone to learn it with rapt attention, in order to be helpful in crossing "Bhavasagara"- the ocean of worldly sorrows and pains and "Ajnyana"- the ignorance! It is said that Vyasa has light up radiant candle of knowledge for the benefit of mankind. It assumes that Gopala – Lord Krishna has milked 'Upanishadic Wisdom" for knowledge-thirsty Arjuna.

Relevance to Modern Professional Life

Smt. Durgabai Bhagwat wrote in the preamble of "Vyasa Parva" in 1962- "With increase in speed and stress of mechanical life, the importance of Gita started going up. Her need was felt desperately, which enhanced its Aura. Seers are constantly in search of immortal places of belief especially after devastating effects of Second World War. Humanity is being questioned and destruction is all around. This is exact resemblance with Mahabharata.

Such great personality (Lord Krishna) is unlikely to take birth again. Hence we should remember and salute these ideals, symbols and ensure that we do not reduce our distance from them."

Naturally one tends to refer to such immortal creations under extreme conditions. While studying Gita, one really gets astonished to see the inner strength and energy of this book, which has not only sustained for centuries, but has become more relevant today than in the past."

ADHAYA (CHAPTER NO.)	TITLE
1(47)	Arjuna Vishada Yoga (Path of Grief)
2(72)	Sankhya Yoga (Path of Light)
3(43)	Karma Yoga (Path of Work)
4(42)	Dnyana Yoga (Path of Knowledge)
5(29)	Karma Sanyasa Yoga (Path of Renunciation)
6(47)	Dhyana Yoga (Path of Meditation)
7(30)	Vidnyana Yoga (Path of Wisdom)
8(28)	Akshara Parabrahma Yoga (Path of Imperishable Supreme Ultimate)
9(34)	Raj Vidya Raj Guhya Yoga (Path of Royal Knowledge and Royal Secret)
10(42)	Vibhuti Yoga (Path of Divine Splendors)
11(55)	Vishwaroopa Darshan Yoga (Path of Universal Vision)
12(20)	Bhakti Yoga (Path of Devotion)
13(34)	Khsetra Khsetragna Yoga (Path of Field and Knower of Field)
14(27)	Guna Yoga (Path of Conduct)
15(20)	Purushttam Prapti Yoga (Path of Super Personhood)
16(24)	Daivasur- Sampad- Vibhaga Yoga(Path of Divine and Devilish Attributes)
17(28)	Shraddha Yoga (Path of Dedication)

18(78)	Moksha- Sanyasa Yoga (Path of Release, Renunciation)

Table: Structure and Composition of Shrimat Bhagwad Gita

EXTRACTS FROM BHAGVAD GITA RELEVANT TO LEADERSHIP CONCEPTS OF MODERN MANAGEMENT

BHAGVAD GITA	MODERN MANAGEMENT
II-3* (Yield not, Partha, to weakness; this is not fit to be feeble like this. Weakness of heart is low, unwise, "Terror of enemies"! Get up and rise!)	Encouraging Leadership (Encouragement energises even during depression.)
II-11 (You grieve for which none should grieve. See my friend! Wise never grieve.)	Present Reality (Accepting what has happened and not worrying about what has not happened is wisdom.)
III-11 (Let the divine wish you well. Let you wish the divine well. Mutually you wish each other well. Reap then best and you live well.)	Mutual Support (Offer and receive.)
III-21 (How behaves the best of men, so behave the rest of men. His example, they will show saying "He did so! We do so!")	Setting own example (Role Model)
III-22 (Partha! For me in three worlds- there are no pending works. None to attain and none to do. Still the work, I always to)	Working Leader (A leader's sign is own work.)

III-26 (Do not disturb the ignorant one, who does the work with attachment. Can show him way, intelligent one by doing well with detachment)	Gentle Teacher (The Intelligent gently lifts the ignorant through persuasion.)
IV-7 (Whenever wherever the right is harmed, Whenever wherever the wrong has formed, when wrong is up and right is down, then Bharata! I come on my own.)	Chaos and Emerging leadership (In chaos a leader emerges through taking responsibility.)
IV-8 (To protect the good and right men, to destroy the evil and wrong of men, to establish the right at each stage, I occur at right time, age by age.)	Establishing Right (A responsible leader corrects wrong and protects right.)
IV-19 (One who starts all his works, completely free from all desires; in fire of knowledge are treated whose works he is called as learned, by seers.)	Knowledge Fire (When work is heat-treated in Knowledge, it is enriching work.)
IV-34 (You may know that from seeing ones, knowledgeable/experienced ones, by approaching and serving them and with respect enquiring them.)	Learning (With knowledge you know the words; with experience you know the meaning.)

IV-39 (Gets knowledge dedicated one, his senses who has won; ultimate peace from knowledge comes, in shorter time promptly it comes.)	**Devoted Master** (A dedicated leader gets a dedicated team.)
IV-42 (Therefore destroy doubts in your heart with knowledge sword in one spurt; established in yoga take a stand. Bharata! Get up and firmly stand.)	**Doubtless Stand** (A doubtless participant is a spotless contributor.)
V-17 (Thinking THAT self in THAT, aligned to THAT and aiming THAT; they attain the non-return path that clean defects in knowledge path.)	**Total Concentration** (Knowledgeable concentration leads to the realisation of excellence.)
VI-5 (Let one lift self by self, let down not self by self; self is best friend of self and self is worst enemy of self.)	**Best Friend** (Mind the mind and be one's best friend.)
VI-29 (All living beings in his self, in all living beings his very self; sees yogi with harmonious self, sameness everywhere for that self.)	**Empathetic Leadership** (Equality is quality.)

VI-40 (Neither in this, and, in that not, harm for him is there not; the doer of good, now you see. My dear Arjuna! Fails not he.)	Reassuring Leadership (It is better to fail in working for a good cause, rather than succeed in working for a wrong cause.)
VII-7 (There is nothing greater than me, there is nothing higher than me; all these worlds are strung on me, like diamonds on strings, now you see.)	Value adding Leadership (Leadership is transforming the group into a valuable team.)
IX-10 (Nature, under supervision of "Me" produces moving, non-moving see! Because of the fact, this very one world revolves then, Kunti's Son)	Super- Vision (Supervision is Super-Vision)
IX-18 (Goal, supporter, lord, witness; me, Shelter, refuge, well-wisher; me, origin and also end in me, treasure, imperishable seed is me)	Roles (A job is what is assigned! A role is what is required!!)
IX-22 (Who worship in none-other way me, who are eternally devoted to me; who are well aligned to me, their welfare, takes care, me)	Welfare (Share and care for people's welfare)

IX-26 (A leaf, flower, fruit or water, may be, with devotion whoever offers to me, that devotee's effortful offering to me, I accept with love, now you see)	Effortless Offerings (With devotion, work is worship)
XI-5 (Partha see forms of me, hundreds and thousands see; different people see different ones, multi shaped, colored ones)	Vision (The visionary conceives the impossible, The missionary makes it possible)
XII-20 (Right way this, immortal way, follows who, this proper way, dedication full, who thinks "me" devoted he is, very dear to me)	Devotion-Love (Dedication creates love and love creates dedication)
XIII-17 (Lights of lights shines everywhere, beyond all darkness, bright everywhere, knowable, knowledge, and its goal seated in all hearts, ultimate goal)	Heartfelt Leadership (Hands, Heels, Heads and Hearts equals Happy Harmonious Humanity)
XVIII-63 (This knowledge was declared to you, secret of secrets by me to you; reflection upon it now fully do you, as per your choice may act you)	Empowering Freedom (Empowerment transforms dedicated team members to responsible leaders)

XVIII-66 (Leaving fully all other ways ye, Take shelter only in me; Removing difficulties all; whole lot, Freedom gives me you grieve not)	Final Point (When there is no way, the leader is the way)
XVIII-78 (Where there is Krishna- the great master, Where there is Arjuna- the great achiever; there- prosperity; success; policy; right, there is also growth that is my sight)	Successful Team (Direction coupled with Dynamism leads to harmonious progress)

***Note- II= Adhaya (Chapter) No. 3= Shloka**

BHAGVAD GITA AND HUMAN RESOURCE DEVELOPMENT

Reference	Description	Relevance
3.43*	Be a warrior, kill desires	Leadership
3.33	Of what use is restrained?	Maturity
3.20	Let your aim be good of all	Integrity
5.21	He is not bound by things	Resourcefulness
8.7	Think of Me at all times	Loyalty
2.2	Strong men know not despair	Adaptability
12.13	Have no thought of 'I" or 'Me"	Team Work
14.23	Remain firm and shake not	Decisiveness
6.17	Attain perfection in whatever you do	Excellence
2.50	Wisdom in work is Yoga	Job Knowledge
2.47	Set your heart upon process	System
6.35	The man in truth can be trained	Development
2.38	Prepare for war with peace in your soul	Competitiveness
3.26	Work with Devotion	Productivity
17.15	Harmony of words is peace, beauty and truth	Communication
18.10	Work, pleasant or painful, is joy	Dignity of Labor

| 2.47 | Action without desire of fruits | Work is Worship |

* Note- 3.43 = Third Adhaya (Chapter), Forty Third Shloka

EXTRACTS FROM BHAGVAD GITA RELEVANT TO TEACHING- LEARNING PROCESS

BHAGVAD GITA	T-L PROCESS
I-47* (When an impending and threatening situation comes in front of a doubtful learner, he gets drowned in the fear of possible disaster and becomes paralyzed with inaction. He gets caught between fear of failure and shame of withdrawal).	Confused Learner
II-1,2 (Responsible teacher is always a compassionate guide who inspires in critical situations. He does hand holding and takes the learner away from the path of depression in a convincing and caring manner.)	Compassionate Teacher
II-3 (Yield not Partha to weakness, this is not fit to be feeble like this! Weakness of heart is low, unwise 'Terror of enemies!" Get up and rise.)	Encouraging Teacher
II-50 (Continuous improvement is the key and path is through 'Yoga"- synthesis of actions, feelings, thoughts and spirit through sincerity, dedication, honesty and nobility.)	Skillful Teacher

III-21 (How behaves the best of men, So behaves the rest of men! His example- they will show, Saying "He did so! So we do so!")	Teacher as example (Role model)
III-22 (Partha! For me in three worlds- There are no pending works, None to attain and none to do, still the work I always do.)	Working Teacher
III-26 (The intelligent teacher gently lifts the ignorant ones through example and persuasion.)	Gentle Teacher
III-42 (The conscious teacher integrates actions with feelings and feelings with thoughts and thoughts with spirit.)	Conscious Teacher
IV-28 (It is studying self in terms of SWOT. This improves internal knowledge, understanding and wisdom.)	Self Study
IV-34 (The three qualities of a good learner are worshipping, serving and gentle enquiring.)	Learning & Teaching
V-17 (Doubt is the cause of inaction and procrastination. The learner has to achieve clarity through information, knowledge, ideas and understanding.)	Total Concentration

VI-5 (Let one lift self by self, Let down not self by self! Self is best friend of self; self is worst enemy of self!!)	Self Development
VI-29 (All living beings in own self, in living beings own very self! Sees Yogi with harmonious self, Sameness everywhere for that self!!)	Empathy
VI-40 (Teacher assures the learners that when the goals and means are correct and when the works are to be undertaken for the benefit of all, there is no possibility of harm even in case of failure.)	Reassuring teacher
VII-7 (Teacher is like a thread in garland, the learners are flowers, and the class is garland.)	Connecting and Value Adding Teacher
XII- 13 to 20 (With good qualities the teacher is not only noble but also is lovable and will be dearly admired by all.)	Loveable Teacher
XIII-17 (When the hearts are joined, the atmosphere of empathy, friendship and love pervades throughout the class and Institution.)	Heartful Teacher

XIV- 5 TO 8, 18 (Sattvik learner is self-disciplined. Rajasik student is aggressive, talkative and authoritative, demands attention. Tamasik student is stubborn, lazy and ignores lessons, exercises, home work and class work. Appropriate relationships with all three categories of learners are hallmarks of Sattvik Teacher.)	Conduct and Character
XV-5 (The spiritual teacher is without desires apart from needs and is internally and externally clean. They practice eternal values and reach infinity.)	Spiritual Teacher
XVI- 1to 5 (A learner on the improvement path avoids and eliminates devilish qualities and acquires and inculcates the divine qualities.)	Divine Qualities
XVIII-63 (This knowledge was declared to you, Secrets of secrets by me to you! Reflection upon it now you fully do, Then as per your choice may act you!!)	Empowering Freedom
XVIII-72 (Partha! Then have you heard? Concentrating mind have you heard? Are you free from ignorance now, delusion too? Oh! Dhananjaya, now how you think?)	Feedback

XVIII-73 (My delusion is destroyed, memory is gained! Achyuta, because of your grace, all is gained. Stable is me and gone are doubts, Now shall act on your words!!)	Inspired and Responsible Learner
XVIII-78 (Where there is Krishna- the great master, where there is Arjuna- the great achiever, There prosperity, success, policy right, There is also growth that is my sight!!)	Successful Partnership

* **Note- I= Adhaya (Chapter) No. 47= Shloka**

CHAPTER 7

Dnyaneshwari (Bhavarth Dipika)

The original version of the Bhagvad Gita was written in Sanskrit by sage Vyasa. But many people could not correctly grasp the essence of the meanings and lessons of this early version. It is believed that for this reason, Sant Dnyaneshwar translated approximately 9000 verses of the holy book to Dnyaneshwari, a Prakrit dialect and an ancestor of the Marathi language.

Dnyanaeshwari is a refined version of the Bhagvad Geeta, with a mixture of rationalism and scientific reasoning to make its doctrines more relevant and practical to modern readers. It is perfect for those readers who seek the path of theology and spirituality through the reasoning of the mind. This is an interpretation of the celestial song "Bhagvad Gita" in an enchanting lilt by India's most revered Saint Dnyaneshwar. It is worth noting that he was just sixteen years of age when the great commentary was written and this extraordinary genius is ascribed to him as being Divine Incarnation Himself(Dnyaneswar is human incarnation of Lord Vishnu)! Lord Krishna is being described as the World Teacher in Dnyaneshwari.

Dnyaneshwari provides the philosophical basis for the Bhagwat Dharma, a Bhakti sect which has a lasting effect on the history of Maharashtra. It is one of the sacred books (i.e. the Prasthanatrai of Bhagwat Dharma) It is one of the foundations of the Marathi language and literature and continues to be widely read in Maharashtra. The Pasayadan or the nine ending verses of the Dnyaneshwari are also popular with the masses.

"My Dnyaneshwari is Godmother of Yogin; she exhibits secrets of sacred Vedic tenets.' –Saint Namdev

This verse demonstrates image of Dnyaneshwari in the thoughts of great contemporary saints, poets and masses about seven hundred years ago. It is the faith of "varkari" devotees that placed Dnyanaehswari not in reading rooms but in their worship rooms as form of God. He rendered Knowledge and ultimate Truth to innumerable Bhaktas that were wandering in the darkness.

"One may beg for survival but should read Dnyanaeshwari" so said great poet saint Tukaram; "It is very nectar of Dnyana and Mukti' he prays. Moreover "the Gita grants blissful enlightenment" he adds. His devotee saint Bahinabai describes it being a unique sculpture in the form of Varkari Temple. According to her, Dnyaneswar laid foundation stone and built the temple whereas Tukaram became its flag post; it gives shelter and succor to everyone seeking Bhakti (Devotion) and Mukti (Deliverance).

These are glimpses of great saints who experienced divinity of Dnyanaeshwar and Dnyaneshwari during their own times. The enchanting divine experience, while reciting Dnyaneshwari remains sublime even today. It is still attractive, puritative and glitterative as Sunshine even after seven hundred years of its first appraisal to masses.

It is an unparalleled creation of Saint Dnyanaeshwar, a Yogin, Saint, Natha and Satshishya of Nivruttinath as well as great poet. It is Veda, Purana, Mantra and scripture leading to Moksha for "varkari". The greatness and nobility of language, the power of expression, astonishing concepts and selection of words are scattered throughout every verse of Dnyaneshwari.

Dnyaneshwar was a Yogi. He appears to be well-versed in all practices of Yoga. Whenever he has spoken of Yoga and its practices he appears to be speaking with so much confidence that we feel that he is speaking not from hear say but from his personal experience. The ultimate live Samadhi, that Dnyaneshwar took, to put an end to his life, shows also that he had full knowledge of the practice of Yoga. Along with Yoga, Dnyaneshwar has not neglected other ways of devotion like "Bhakti" and worship of the idol of the God. He has done enough justice to all these whenever necessary and has also described their importance in human life.

From the point of view of the development of Rasas, Dnyaneshwari is not wanting. In the eleventh canto when Lord Krishna shows to Arjuna the whole universe, we see the development of different Rasas like Rowdra, Bhayanaka, and Shanta etc. This also shows that Dnyaneshwar had studied the books on literary criticism that were existing at his time.

Dnyaneshwari is supposed to be the basic book of the. "Varkari" sect. Every "Varkari "who recognises God Vitthal as his God reveres this book unequivocally. In all the lectures of these people they will be constantly referring to "Ovis "from this highly revered book. Apart from the followers of the Varkari Sect, other great Marathi Saints like Namdeo, Eknath, Tukaram, and Ramdas have always mentioned Dnyaneshwari with reverence, and have taken pride in stating that they have been the followers of Dnyaneshwar. Most of the Marathi poets who wrote on religious subjects have made free use of the similes, ideas and quotations from Dnyaneshwari, and even acknowledged that they got inspiration to write their books after reading it.

As Bhagvad Gita has been the source of inspiration for writing a criticism to many Marathi poets, similarly there have also been a number of books in Marathi for explaining the philosophy of Dnyaneshwari. As nearly 700 years have elapsed since the composition of Dnyaneshwari, its language has become obscure at certain places, some of the words used therein cannot be understood by the modern generation, and hence the modern generation is mostly not able to read or understand Dnyaneshwari without a commentary or a guide.

Saint Dnyaneshwar in Dnyaneshwari is not giving importance to words, impressions and structure of Gita. For him what is significant is the message, experiences given by Gita to senses. Spirituality, philosophy, prose and poetry are the pillars of Marathi seen in Dnyaneshwari. But this is just the tip of iceberg.

"Dnyaneshwari has created base for Marathi culture. If we consider saint Namdev, saint Tukaram, Justice Ranade and Acharya Vinoba Bhave as four stages of Marathi culture then essentially the foundation of all is laid down by Saint Dnyaneshwar."

Saint Dnyaneshwar himself has described Dnyaneshwari as "Dharma Kirtan" (by Dharma he meant action, duty). But the basis of duty has to be spirituality. Dnyaneshwari does not pray for running away from life, laziness or sacrificing family, but it insists for universal orientation, detachment and duty boundedness. People of Maharashtra are not known for polite language and behaviour but Dnyaneshwari is an exception to this, primarily because it represents personality of the creator, Saint Dnyaneshwar, himself.

No one will find hatred, evil or revengeful language in this book, but it is full of all encompassing personality, mature understanding of human life and above all empathy. This makes Dnyanaeshwari different from other literature. Saint Dnyaneshwar is praying for entire universe and its well being. People say that we all are alone here. But saint Dnyanaeshwar disagrees with this. According to Dnyaneshwar, each one of us is full of spiritual system. Those who show path to such individuals are "Saints" according to him. Saints alone can bring harmony, can improve relations and enable getting rid of evil.

Dnyaneshwari appeals to inner layers of communication, coordination and cooperation between all elements of this universe so that we can destroy darkness from our lives leading to Karma. Symbol of such harmonious universe is the Saint.

Dnyaneshwari is written as per chapters of Bhagvad Gita. It has number to respective verse so as to simplify learning process. Simple and easy to understand examples are given for the benefit of common readers. In the third chapter, Dnyaneshwar dwells upon Dnyana Yoga and Karma Yoga. Lord Krishna gives his own example to Arjuna while explaining the concept of Swadharma. He says, I have nothing to achieve, still I follow swadharma, so that I can set an example for others. If I stop working, then the entire world will come to stand still. Krishna explains that the one, who knows me, gets salvation. Those who follow Yama-Niyama get automatically purified and thus become part of "Me."

While defining Karma with the help of Dnyaneshwari, it is evident that the creator of this world is Karma. Dnyani are those who never expect fruits of their deeds and are busy in performing their duties. Lord in the forth chapter gives types of yagnya- Dravya Yagnya (Performed by donation of money), Wag Yagnya (Performed with the help of words)., Dnyana Yagnya, Yoga Yagnya and Tapo Yagnya. While advising Arjuna, Lord says, if by merely reciting Mantra, the enemy dies, then why to carry sword? If cure is possible by eating sweets, then why to drink something that tastes extremely bad? In fifth chapter Dnyanaeshwar says, rays may be different, but light remains same. Just like in the light of lamp, we can perform household activities, our organs work in the presence of eternal spirit. Next Dnyaneshwar says, even if sun rises in the east, light is spread across all directions. This is the simplicity of Dnyanaeshwari. Such day to day life examples enable ordinary and illiterate people to understand and appreciate it. In the sixth chapter, various chakras have been described in a lucid language. Further, Lord advices that all bodily pleasures should be controlled. If these external processes (eating, sleeping etc) are well managed, then internal happiness increases. Although good medicine can cure our diseases, our tongue creates a problem by not swallowing that medicine. Like this all eighteen chapters of Gita are covered by Dnyaneshwari.

Finally Dnyanaeshwar concludes with Pasayadan, the famous blessings which he has urged for the wellbeing of entire mankind. This is what precisely HR Managers and top management of any organisation prays /attempts for wellbeing of its employees.

STRUCTURE AND COMPOSITION OF DNYANESHWARI

ADHAYA (CHAPTER NO.)	TITLE
1(275)	" Arjun Vishada Yoga " (Despondency of Arjuna)
2(375)	Sankhya and Yoga
3(276)	Karma Yoga
4(225)	" Dnyana- Karma- Sanyasa Yoga" (Sankhya Yoga)
5(180)	" Karma- Sanyasa Yoga" (Renunciation)
6(497)	" Atma- Sayyam Yoga" (Dhyana Yoga)
7(210)	" Dnyana- Vidnyana Yoga" (Wisdom and Knowledge)
8(271)	" Akshara- Brahma Yoga " (The imperishable Brahman)
9(535)	" Rajavidya- Rajaguhya Yoga " (The Esoteric Knowledge)
10(335)	" Vibhooti Yoga" (The Divine Manifestation)
11(708)	" Vishvaroopa- Darshan Yoga " (The Universal Form)
12(247)	Bhakti Yoga
13(1169)	" Kshetra- Kshetrajnya- Vibhag Yoga " (The Field and the Knower of the Field)
14(415)	" Gunatraya- Vibhaga Yoga " (The Three Qualities)

15(599)	" Purushottama- Yoga " (The Supreme Person)
16(473)	" Daivasur- Sampad- Vibhaga Yoga " (The Divine and Demoniacal Nature)
17(433)	" Shraddhatraya- Vibhaga Yoga " (Three Kinds of Faith)
18(1810)	" Moksha- Sanyasa Yoga " (Release)

Note- Figure in bracket indicates no. of Ovis in the respective chapter.

RELEVANCE OF TEACHINGS & WRITINGS OF SAINT DNYANESHWAR TO MODERN PROFESSIONAL LIFE

Chapter / Ovi	Meaning	Reference
9/377	One should leave aside all "greatness" as well as ego of scholarship and become humble than humblest.	**Egolessness**
3/157	Whatever a great man does, others also do the same; whatever standard he sets for himself, the people follow that!	**Role Model**
1/62	A person with steady mind and profound can be saint.	**Attributes of Saints**
18/1225-26	The wind scatters the cloud, which cover the sun, but cannot create the sun. The moss can be set aside from the water by hand, but one cannot create water. In that way, the scripture can remove the dirt of ignorance, which obscures the knowledge of self.	**Removal of irrational beliefs**
3/148	The need for action remains only until one acquires Knowledge of the Self.	**Importance of action**
6/378	If the intellect has strong support of fortitude, it brings the mind gradually on the path of self-realisation and establishes it in the temple of the Supreme Self.	**Mind Management**

15/272	Like tongue tasting itself, or eye seeing itself, one should be able to view one's own self, leaving aside entire duality.	**Self-Realisation (Awareness-Acceptance-Analysis-Application)**
16/198	While the body engages in selfless activities outwardly, his conscience is full of Viveka (discretion) within, such a person is purity personified inside out for certain. Disinterested activities and discrimination of the mind are the signs of external and internal purity.	**Fortitude**
6/67-70	One should raise oneself up through the self (mind), and never debase oneself; for verily mind alone is his friend and mind alone is his enemy.	**Self-Development**
14/312	If a serpent casts away its slough and enters the nether region (pit), who is there to take care of this discarded slough?	**Seer**
14/387	Unique and enriched conviction that one is not different from Lord and one verily remains as Lord alone verily means Bhakti(Devotion)	**Bhakti (Devotion)**
9/188	Righteousness regains in his good thoughts and desires and his mind always nourishes discriminating knowledge.	**Empathy and Rationality**

16/159-160	Just as a shooting of pain resulting from a prick of a thorn, registers itself on one's face, one should feel compassion at the suffering of others. Just as the eyes benefit from the cooling sensation of the sole, one should be happy by seeing others happy.	**Empathy**
12/120	Just as the water follows the course as devised by the gardener, one should also perform given action.	**Change Acceptance**
5/73	One should perform actions as others who have the motive of reward, but remains indifferent to it with the notion that he is not its agent. (as if not done at all)	**Karma Yoga**
18/357-358	Once the goals are clear, mind's resolve is verbalised through speech. The mind is the instrumental cause of decision of action. This decision finds expression in speech and then in the light of that speech, the way of action (Karma-Path) becomes clear and agent undertakes that action. The doer (Karta) is induced into activity.(Kartrutva).	**Desires lead to Purpose**

14/265-269	The Sattva is the cause of knowledge, as the sun is the cause of the day. Similarly greed is caused by Rajas quality. The Tamas quality gives rise to the three faults of delusion, ignorance and heedlessness. Out of the three, rajas and tamas lead to a man's fall, while the sattva alone conduces the knowledge.	**Sattva, Rajas & Tamas qualities in human**
14/290	An actor plays different roles with great skills, but is not deceived thereby and knows he is mere witness.	**Self- Image**
13/474	One who has cleansed his exterior by pious works and removed the internal stains by knowledge becomes purified inside out. Just as a light in a pane of glass is seen to move inside, so his pure thoughts become manifest in the activities of his sense organs.	**Reflection of emotions through actions**

CHAPTER 8

Tukaram Gatha

In the reprint of Gatha, it is admitted that literature of Saints is immortal. It is an important treasure of our life. The saints have played vital role in developing individuals, society and nations. Through the writings these saints showed us path of humanity by crossing all boundaries of caste, creed, and religion. That is why even after so many centuries people are still attached to the teachings and writings of Marathi Saints. Saints have established social and spiritual equality, humanity and taught us good behaviour. The society has remained intact despite so many disasters because of this strong foundation led by saints. This work is beyond description. Dnyanaeshwari, Gatha and Dasbodh are not merely studied but are practiced in day to day life. We could strength societal growth and change process was accelerated. Any knowledge, when supported by spirituality and values becomes constructive and benefits mankind.

Teachings and writings of saints are a natural and continuous flow of energy.

Saint Tukaram struggled throughout his life. All that he suffered has appeared in his Abhangas. In one way it is his biography, self-narration and also thought process. His Abhangas have clarity of thoughts, simple language, and antidotes which enrich our life.

Another characteristic of his Abhangas is that they are the voice of socially exploited, down trodden class of society. Hence they are integral part of daily readings of large section of society. Maharashtra Government, on the occasion of completion of three hundred years of writing of Gatha, in 1950 took initiative to print it for the first time.

It is prayed that the teachings and writings of saints should continue to be guiding lamps for mankind thereby united; strong and enriched society can be built.

Maharashtra has been fortunate enough that the shelter of association of saints is on going for last so many centuries. Despite lot of physical and technological developments, we still continue to be attached to these saints. Maharashtra could retain its identity and culture only because of spiritual work and we really need to be grateful to the saints.

We occasionally find reference to the castes in this literature but it is primarily owing to the prevalent structure of the society otherwise the saints only practiced what they preached and took the entire society to next level. Abhangas of Tukaram reflect farmers and their livelihood through various examples and stories. Only Saint Tukaram can simplify human life in such lucid language and attract common man towards spiritualisation. His literary work also has social education as an important component. He strongly opposed evil traditions and customs of society and revolutionised society around him.

No one to this day has satisfactorily solved all the questions that crop up in regard to Tukaram's poetry- compositions, for instance, as to what was the total number of Abhangs that he wrote, how many of them are available at present, whether some of the Abhangs that bear the name of Tuka are not really the work of some other person of that name, and so on.

Popularity of Tukaram's poetry has never abated in the least to this day, no bhajan possible without it, and there can be no kirtan but must begin with it and end with it-with the Abhang "Grant just this, O Lord !".Several lines of his writings have become household words! No other Marathi poet, medieval or modern, has ever had such universal allegiance. Since the Government compilation, there have appeared about twenty-five editions of Tukaram's Abhangs during the last sixty years published by various publishers, the total number of their copies amounting to well-nigh a hundred thousand. Most of these, however, are mere reprints of other collections.

To review and assess the worth of the poetry of Tukaram would be the height of presumption for any but his compeers like Dnyanaeshwar, Namdev, Ekanath, and other saints. The poetry having bubbled forth from the deepest recesses of the saint's heart cannot be easily valued by an ordinary mortal. The saint's expression of his ideas is unsparingly outspoken, yet overflowing with love. One critic may regard the language used in certain places as 'harsh', another may point to his outspokenness in certain places as 'indecent', a third may object that certain words he has used are 'vulgar'. As literature, Tukaram's poetry is wholly spiritual and introspective and can well be compared and contrasted with the poetry it bears the closest resemblance. The poetical merit of Dnyanaeshwar's work, especially in respect of the Dnyaneshwari, is very high, its language also is highly 'urbane', that is to say, courteous and elegant. Even when he wants to thrash, Dnyanaeshwar does so with a silken string of delicate words, so that the lashes, far from causing smarting pain, only produce a tickling sensation. Not so Tukaram. He has, as it were, a leather strap ready to lay on the backs of people. This difference was natural in away, for while Dnyanaeshwar was primarily an author, Tukaram was an out and out preacher, admonishing people face to face! Tukaram's poetry, however, has one important peculiarity: when it comes to the invoking of Shri Pandurang, its harshness disappears, and it is all a smooth-flowing stream of sweetness and love! Tukaram, on occasions, did not dare to 'quarrel' with Pandurang Himself, but the words that he uses there are so ingenious that they were calculated to provoke in the Deity not anger but only a smile! Tukaram's similes are very expressive and sweet. His language, though somewhat rustic, is both striking and effective. It is apparently very simple, but the meaning of some of the Abhangs is not easy to grasp. The variety of abhangs adds to the difficulty still further. Tukaram firmly believed that his verse was not his own, that his mouth was merely a vehicle for Shri Pandurang's utterance.

Tukaram's Abhangs, barring a few incidental ones, can be roughly classified under the following topics;

1. The Puranas (Mythology);

2. Lives of Saints;

3. Panegyric of Shri Pandurang;

4. Laudatory description of Pandharpur;

5. Autobiography and self-scrutiny;

6. Moral Instructions

7. Personal Explanations

8. Miscellaneous

9. In defense of his Religious Principles and

10. Bharud (Mixed)

Besides Abhangs, Tukaram has a considerable quantity of other verse in a variety of forms, such as Shlok, Arati and Gaulani.

His sense of oneness is not limited to mankind, but is wide enough to embrace the whole living and sentient world, as is evidenced by the use of the word 'being', instead of 'man' in these Abhangs.

Though Tukaram was not a great scholar like Dnyanaeshwar, Ekanath, Vaman and others, his reading of books and observation of men and things was, for his time, considerable indeed, as shown by his writings. His formal education had never gone beyond reading and writing; yet, once his mind had turned towards spiritual life, he made large additions to his knowledge by reading several Marathi works on Puranas and philosophy, by getting a number of Sanskrit books explained to him, and by attending performances of kirtan and reading of Puranas. Dnyaneshwari and the Bhagwat of Ekanath formed the solid basis of his poetry. The profundity of his knowledge of the world and of human nature can easily be gauged from the hundreds of topics that he has dealt with, as occasion demanded, in his Abhangs. They give a good deal of information regarding the state of society, religion and country prevailing at the time.

Even as mere poetical compositions, his Abhangs rank high. He never made any conscious attempt at composing in strict conformity with the canons of the science of poetics. But his feelings were so powerful that verses composed by him under their influence would automatically become the highest kind of genuine poetry.

RELEVANCE OF TEACHINGS & WRITINGS OF SAINT TUKARAM TO MODERN PROFESSIONAL LIFE

Abhang No.	Meaning
37	You will reap wholesome fruits if you sow a pure seed. He, who speaks sweet honeyed words, puts his body to good work and has a mind as pure as Ganga, relieves you of your sorrows and agony on casting a look at him.
38	He, who maintains equanimity of mind, instead of becoming miserable in the bad time of his life, learns lesson from there. Thus he transforms even bad time of his life into gold. There could be no good of a person who has a mind full of cravings. If the temperature of the body has gone up due to mental agony then there is no use of applying sandalwood to the body.
268	There is no happiness greater than the peace of mind. Everything else causes sorrow. Therefore make your mind peaceful to see the inner light. One with a mind agitated by anger and lust has to suffer ensuing restlessness. A peaceful mind is free from such sufferings.
745	It is better to be low profile. When a river is flooded even the mightiest of the trees falls by its force. But the humble grass on its shores remains intact. If we bow before the mighty wave of an ocean it passes over our head without any harm. If we grasp the feet of a very mighty enemy then his might cannot work.
1287	Remove ego from your head, you will feel relieved. You will also be free from the vice of lust and anger.

1446	Before grinding grains of wheat into flour, stones should be thrown out after scrutiny. Otherwise the flour will be spoiled. Similarly grass should be weeded out to get good harvest of the crop. This policy should be applied while dealing with bad elements in the society. He, who forgets this policy, is put to a loss.
1507	He, who eats an onion, acquires smell worse than that of an onion. Similarly he, who keeps in the company of evil, faces more severe consequences.
1513	He, who drinks wine for pacifying his mind, immediately loses balance of his mind. Whatever may be the intentions, company of bad persons cannot bring anything good.
1544	He, who speaks the truth, becomes sad at the sight of other's sorrow, gets good results of his actions.
1960	Let us help each other on the noble path.
2003	The best sacrifice is the sacrifice of ego. He, who sacrifices the ego, neither craves for happy moments nor shows any aversion for the adverse time.
2085	Earn money through an honest business. Spend money for noble cause by maintaining equanimity of mind. Work for others' welfare. Don't say harsh words for others. Consider others' ladies like your mother and sisters. Show kindness to all beings. Make possible arrangements for drinking water at remote places for quenching the thirst of people. Don't harm others. He, who abides by the above teaching, spreads good name of his parents all around.

2113	The Sun absorbs vapors of every kind of water but it remains unaffected by the quality of water. Similarly while giving light the Sun does not discriminate among creatures.
2398	In the pond of happiness, there are ripples of happiness.
2479	Whatever pressure is there on the mind, it is causing much uneasiness. Later one finds through experience that the pressure was not that much disturbing as was made out to be.
2968	Respect and place in a society does not come free of cost. One has to wear out for its gain.
2994	Jealousy to others, cruel mind, taking extreme positions is the sign of being evil. Whatever is in the mind that manifests itself in the behaviour? Good people always have regard to the time while behaving. They are always equanimous and pure.
3149	Don't rejoice at others misery. For a moment you may feel happy but later on you will suffer. Abstain from such thinking that is sinful. Jealousy having taken roots in the mind will lead to a total disaster. Anger reduces stock of virtues. Whatever happens that does happen due to the effect of our past actions.
3150	He whose devotion is for making money, what knowledge he can gain? He is meditating with his mind full of lust, how God can reside in his mind? He keeps his eyes on fruits of work; can he ever be united with the God? His mind is always engrossed with sensual subjects, whether he can understand the God?

CHAPTER 9

Dasbodh

Introduction by Samarth himself about structure and contents of Dasbodh:

"Dasbodh contains dialogue between the Guru and his disciples. The path of devotion is clearly explained in it. According to Samarth, he has explained the nine ways of devotion, the path of knowledge, the qualities inherent in the state of desirelessness, and also explained are the various facets of spiritual life. The book makes definite statements about the real nature of essence of devotion, the pure nature of knowledge and the real state of being, the Self. This book also tells definitely what the purest teaching is, what complete freedom is and the meaning of attainment of liberation. It states in clear terms a) what is the nature of Reality within, b) what is the state of being beyond body-consciousness and c) what it means to be alone in this world. This book tells who is the supreme Almighty God, who is the real devotee, what are the Jeeva- the soul and the Shiva- the universal spirit. In this book it is definitely stated what is the nature of the Absolute Brahman, with an explanation of all the doctrines about it. It also gives the main types of worship, various forms of poetry and various kinds of shrewd discernment. This book explains how illusion itself comes into being, the details of five elements and who is the Doer of all things. Many doubts are cleared, many misunderstandings are removed and many problems are solved by removing objections. So it may be said that Dasbodh gives many facets of knowledge. Further Samarth says that the whole volume of Dasbodh is divided into Twenty Dashakas which are groups of ten chapters each. Each such Dashaka contains lucidly explained separate subjects.

It is worth mentioning here that the book is supported by many authentic ancient works like Vedas, Upanishads and Gita plus personal experience is the main parameter relied upon, which is supported by the doctrines of the scriptures. Now about the benefits of listening to this book- first is that there is immediate transformation in the behaviour of the listener. Another is ignorance, sorrow and illusion are destroyed and wisdom is attained. Desirelessness which is the greatest fortune of Yogis is inculcated in our very life; and wisdom with discrimination is easily understood. Those who are having illusion, bad qualities/ attitude become endowed with virtue. Those who have acute discernment, and are logical in thinking come to understand the proprieties of timely behaviour. Those who are idle become earnest, the sinners repent, and critics start praising the path of devotion. Those who are in bondage become aspirants for freedom, fools become very alert and those who are not devotees, actually follow the path of devotion and attain liberation. Many vices are destroyed, the downfallen become pure and by listening, man advances towards the highest state. By listening deeply to the contents of this book, many dangers involved in the attachment to physical body and many misgivings and sufferings of the worldly life are destroyed. Such is the benefit- by listening, one is saved from downfall and his mind becomes content and peaceful."

"Each big, stable and organised group of people has its own personality. Maharashtra, which is showcasing tradition of knowledge and life style based on it also, has its own personality. All Marathi psychologists have given utmost importance to Bhakti as virtue of life. Marathi saints have the base of Upanishads. The saints have always felt that by nature, every human being is goal oriented and hence tries to chase such goal. The three pillars of Bhakti as narrated in Gita namely Intellect, Humanity and Practicality are taken forward by Marathi Saints. Hence the concept of Bhakti as enumerated by Marathi saints is goal oriented and at the same time respecting mankind.

Samarth has taken forward Bhakti path sighted by Gita and subsequently by Saint Dnyaneshwar in Dnyaneshwari. Samarth believed that in personal life wealth and in spiritual life salvation is the Bhakti Path. According to Samarth, one can have three obstacles in this journey- (1) Karma likely to take back seat which calls for action orientation. (2) Thoughts are likely to be stagnant; hence there is need for creativity. (3) The concentration power is likely to seize in public, hence Samarth insists that while chanting Name, try to spend some time alone. (Away from People- "Lokanta")

When we look at Samarth- his life and his philosophy, we can infer that in Maharashtra, both Dnyanaeshwari and Dasbodh kept spirituality alive. Saints do not stop after self-realisation, but work day and night through their teachings and writings to bring same experience to the people around them. Samarth Ramdas is embodiment of knowledge, bhakti, divinity, peace, and literature. Samarth believed that our behaviour, reading, writing, and action should be of highest level. Life must have magnanimity and beauty filled in it, was his dream.

Emperors in Samarth's days had their own ideas, thoughts, virtues, goals, ethics and policies to rule this country. This had huge impact on society. Short sighted people with selfish motives started running the show. Evil and destructive mental set ups came on surface to further ruin the society. Competition for power, greed for money, hatred started open play. Stability, security took a back seat. Fear, anxiety and instability became talk of the town.

On this backdrop, Samarth wanted to create responsible leadership. Such leaders can bring happiness and smile to the society, will give equal opportunity to cherish ethics which is possible only if these leaders have spiritual foundation. Mahanta, as envisioned by Samarth is Bhakta first and then leader, hence the basis of leadership should be spirituality and ethics. Such leaders have detachment as an important quality. People need to unite, to realise any social goal. Such team should be disciplined and goal oriented. For that new institution needs to be built first. Samarth did exactly same thing.

Dasbodh is in verse form and is very simple and easy to understand. Dasbodh comprises of Twenty Dashaka, Two Hundred Samasa and total seven thousand seven hundred fifty one verses. Spirituality is the atman of Dasbodh. The philosophy can be summarised as follows- (1) while writing Dasbodh, he wrote only based on his experiences. (2) Prior to starting composing Dasbodh, he had studied all philosophical literature written by earlier philosophers. (3) He was totally 'Adwaiti".(Non-dualism) (4) The very reason for writing Dasbodh was establishing connection between visible universe and real nature of human life.

Dasbodh is conversation between Guru and disciples. Samarth has answered one or more questions, doubts raised by disciples in each Samasa. Many a times, Samarth himself has answered couple of queries, which are likely to be raised (similar to FAQ). In the course of narration, we find his personal experiences both practical and spiritual at many places."

Samarth started writing Dasbodh in 1632 and completed the book after 48 years i. e. in 1680. 'Dasbodh' was written in three stages. Samarth wrote this book after he studied behaviour of people around him all over India. Along with other behavioural matters this book guides us in to present Management concepts. Though it was written 350 years back, Samarth with his vast experience has given hints for Leaders, which are even useful today in modern Leadership practices. Samarth Ramdas's 48 years deep thinking, experience and observations are clearly visible in Dasbodh.

The scripture is a great composition of spiritual and behavioural visionary thoughts and wisdom and full of enlightening and strong messages regarding "Working Hard and Working Smart" and for Leadership & Self-Development. Since Samarth Ramdas was not only the Saint but also was the Great Leader and Organiser of his time who created his organisation of 1100 Muths / Centres which were spread over not only in Maharashtra but in many other parts of India. In this process, he created a gigantic work-force of lakhs of volunteers for his social and spiritual objectives in a very systematic and organised way using spiritual and management principles and also created leadership of thousands of able leaders through training and motivation.

Therefore, in 'DASBODH', the great vision of Samarth Ramdas is seen very clearly regarding self-development, leadership qualities and attitudes for positive work-culture and self-learning, which is very useful even in our modern organisation and modern life.

"Das" means servant i.e. a devotee. Ramdas was a devotee of Ram. "Bodh" means "teaching".

In 'Dasbodh', Ramdas touches multiple topics connected to human life.

The book is a beautiful guide for the ideal human life. It teaches us how to shape our life through Ramdas's excellent practical and spiritual principles.

Dasbodh also explains multiple facets of the Universe. It really covers the whole cosmos. Ramdas, however, emphasises the existence of God very strongly and shows common people the easy way to reach God, namely,

'Bhaktimarg'. This, according to him, is a sure path to achieve peace of mind in life.

Samarth realised that the base of a firm and healthy society is a harmonious family. One should not neglect his family. He should fulfill his duties first; otherwise, he is not fit for devoting himself to God.

Samarth handles in "Dasbodh" varied themes, for example, family planning, health, body facts, architecture, construction of buildings, administration, politics, time management, personal development, how to train managers and leaders, management of your own mind and spiritual thoughts. Even Gandhi and Vivekananda had read Dasbodh and had written words of praise on "Dasbodh".

"Dasbodh the magnum opus by Swami Ramdas is an early effort in which ideas on management abound. Except for the early work by a few noteworthy scholars, no attention has been paid to its contents from the management point of view".

STRUCTURE AND COMPOSITION OF DASBODH

DASHAKA NO.	TITLE & CONTENTS
1.	**Prayers**
1.1 (38)	Beginning of the Book
1.2(30)	Hymns in praise of Lord Ganesh
1.3(26)	Praise to Goddess Sharada
1.4(31)	Praise to Spiritual Teacher
1.5(26)	In praise of the Saints
1.6(23)	In praise of Listeners
1.7(34)	Praise of Great Poets
1.8(29)	Praise of Congregation
1.9(27)	In praise of Spiritual Path
1.10(62)	Uniqueness of Human Body
2	**Signs of Fools**
2.1(74)	The Signs of Fools
2.2(42)	Signs of Good Qualities
2.3(40)	Signs of Wrong Knowledge
2.4(27)	Discourse on Devotion
2.5(42)	Rajas- The Quality of Over-activity
2.6(41)	The Tamas Quality
2.7(88)	Sattwa Quality
2.8(32)	Good Knowledge

2.9(43)	The Qualities of Ascetics
2.10(41)	Signs of Educated Fools
3	**Commentary on Life**
3.1(53)	Suffering at birth
3.2(65)	The Misery of Family Life (1)
3.3(48)	The Misery of Family Life (2)
3.4(54)	The Misery of Family Life (3)
3.5(56)	The Misery of Family Life (4)
3.6(56)	Physical Ailments
3.7(87)	Troubles due to Outer Objects
3.8(29)	Cosmic Troubles
3.9(59)	Description of Death
3.10(74)	Asceticism
4	**Nine fold Devotion (Nava- Vidha Bhakti)**
4.1(35)	Listening
4.2(31)	Kirtan- Stories about God
4.3(25)	Remembering Lord Vishnu
4.4(26)	Service to the feet of the Guru
4.5(33)	Worship
4.6(25)	Bowing down to God
4.7(28)	Service
4.8(32)	Friendliness
4.9(30)	Self-Surrender

4.10(31)	The Four States of Liberation
5	**Mantras**
5.1(46)	The Importance of Guru
5.2(73)	Signs of Guru
5.3(104)	Signs of a Disciple
5.4(36)	Signs of Good Teaching
5.5(39)	Knowledge
5.6(75)	Pure Knowledge
5.7(49)	The Signs of a Man in Bondage
5.8(44)	The Signs of the Aspirant
5.9(62)	The Signs of the Seeker
5.10(45)	The Signs of the Master
6	**Search of God**
6.1(31)	Search of God
6.2(45)	Attainment of Brahman
6.3(37)	Appearance of Maya
6.4(24)	Discourse on Brahman
6.5(26)	Discourse on Reality and Illusion
6.6(60)	Discourse on Creation
6.7(45)	Devotion to God with Attributes
6.8(50)	Dissolution of the Visible World
6.9(34)	Search of the Essential
6.10(61)	The Indescribable

7	**Fourteen Brahmans**
7.1(60)	Introduction
7.2(55)	Discourse on Brahman
7.3(53)	The Fourteen Brahmans
7.4(52)	Discourse on Pure Brahman
7.5(44)	Discarding the concept of Duality
7.6(65)	The Difference between the Bound and the Free
7.7(74)	The Importance of Right Efforts
7.8(50)	The Importance of Listening
7.9(60)	The Importance of Listening(2)
7.10(50)	Discourse on Death
8	**The Beginning of Maya**
8.1(60)	The Glimpse of God
8.2(55)	A Subtle Query
8.3(67)	A Subtle Query (2)
8.4(60)	The Subtle Five Elements
8.5(70)	The Differences in the Five Manifest Elements
8.6(54)	Depression
8.7(66)	The Nature of Freedom
8.8(70)	The Vision of Atman
8.9(60)	The Signs of Siddha (Adept)
8.10(82)	Going Beyond The Void

9	**Qualities and the Form**
9.1(29)	Questions
9.2(41)	Discourse on Brahman
9.3(45)	Discourse on Doubtlessness
9.4(44)	Discourse on Knowledge
9.5(41)	Discarding Guesswork
9.6(54)	Description of Qualities and Forms
9.7(57)	Removal of Doubts
9.8(38)	Discourse on Death
9.9(41)	Removal of Doubts
9.10(37)	The Discourse on the State of Atman
10	**The Universal Flame**
10.1(31)	The Oneness of Consciousness
10.2(25)	Doubt about Physical Body
10.3(21)	Clearance of Doubt about Physical Body
10.4(46)	The Nature of the Seed
10.5(28)	The Five Types of Dissolution
10.6(40)	The Nature of Illusion
10.7(31)	The Devotion to the Embodied God
10.8(34)	The Importance of Actual Experience
10.9(30)	Realisation
10.10(68)	Discourse on the Fixed and the Moving
11	**Bheema- Dashaka**

11.1(44)	The Main Doctrine
11.2(40)	The Description of four Manifestation of God
11.3(30)	"The Teaching"
11.4(30)	Discourse on Discrimination
11.5(27)	Discourse on Politics
11.6(19)	The Signs of a "Mahanta"
11.7(22)	The Ever-Moving River
11.8(25)	The Nature of the Antaratman
11.9(25)	The Advice
11.10(25)	The Behaviour of Desire less Man
12	**Discrimination And Desire less Ness**
12.1(20)	The Signs of a Pure Person
12.2(30)	Discourse on Practical Experience
12.3(33)	Signs of a Devotee
12.4(20)	Discrimination and Desire less Ness
12.5(22)	Self- Surrender
12.6(31)	The Sequence of Creation
12.7(31)	Renunciation of Sense-objects
12.8(34)	The Description of Time
12.9(30)	The Teaching about Right Effort
12.10(43)	The Signs of the Best Man
13	**Name and Form**
13.1(31)	Atman and Non-Atman

13.2(30)	Discrimination between the Essence and the Dross
13.3(22)	The Creation
13.4(24)	The Dissolution
13.5(25)	A Story (An allegory)
13.6(31)	Summary of the Teaching
13.7(30)	The Verification by Experience
13.8(38)	The Discourse about who is the Doer
13.9(40)	The Explanation About Atman
13.10(29)	The Teaching
14	**Constant Meditation**
14.1(80)	Signs of a Desire less Person
14.2(22)	The Importance of Charitable Begging
14.3(54)	Discourse on Poetry
14.4(35)	How to perform Kirtan
14.5(41)	The Best Harikatha
14.6(33)	The Signs of Cleverness
14.7(40)	The Present "Times"
14.8(49)	Constant Meditation
14.9(31)	Discourse on the Eternal
14.10(21)	Discourse on Maya
15	**Atma-Dashaka**
15.1(35)	Signs of Shrewdness

15.2(30)	Description of the Work of a Selfless Person
15.3(30)	Discourse on the Inner Atman
15.4(31)	Discourse on Eternal Brahman
15.5(32)	Discourse on the Moving Principle
15.6(30)	Discourse on Cleverness
15.7(42)	The Discourse about " the Above and the Below"
15.8(40)	The Discourse on Small Jeevas
15.9(34)	The Birth of Body
15.10(33)	The Discourse on the Doctrine taught by Teachers
16	**The Sequence of Sevens**
16.1(21)	Praise of Valmiki
16.2(22)	Praise of the Sun
16.3(30)	Praise of the Earth
16.4(31)	Description of Water
16.5(30)	Description of Fire
16.6(34)	In Praise of Air (Wind)
16.7(43)	"The Great Element"(Mahat-Bhoota)
16.8(31)	Discourse on Atman who is God Rama
16.9(29)	Various paths of God-Realisation
16.10(31)	" The Description of the Qualities and the Elements"

17		**The Prakriti and Purusha**
17.1(30)		The Divine Power
17.2(34)		Shiva and Shakti
17.3(30)		The Importance of Listening
17.4(31)		Discarding the way of Guesswork
17.5(24)		The "SOHAM"
17.6(32)		Body-Attachment
17.7(30)		Life of People in the World
17.8(34)		Discourse on Various Elements
17.9(22)		The Four Bodies
17.10(30)		Signs of Stupid Persons
18		**Description of Various Objects**
18.1(24)		Many Deities and their Locations
18.2(30)		The need to consult the Man of Wisdom
18.3(20)		Discourse on How one should be Desire less
18.4(40)		The Importance of Human Body
18.5(33)		The signs of Luckless Persons
18.6(22)		The signs of The Best Man
18.7(20)		The nature of Ordinary People
18.8(25)		Description of the Inner God
18.9(24)		Description about the state of people in sleep
18.10(50)		Bad type of Listeners

19	**The Teaching**	
19.1(20)	Discourse on Art of Writing	
19.2(23)	Instructions for Good Behaviour	
19.3(30)	Discourse on the Signs of a Luckless Person	
19.4(31)	Discourse on the Sings of a Fortunate Person	
19.5(30)	Importance of Body	
19.6(30)	Discourse on Intellectual Differences	
19.7(30)	Discourse on Effort	
19.8(30)	Discourse on Enterprises	
19.9(31)	Discourse on Politics	
19.10(30)	Discourse on the signs of Discrimination of a Mahanta	
20	**Dashaka of Completion**	
20.1(30)	The discourse on the Complete and the Incomplete	
20.2(30)	The Triple Creation	
20.3(30)	The Subtle Terms	
20.4(30)	Discourse on Atman	
20.5(30)	The Four Divisions of Creation	
20.6(30)	Discourse on the Qualities of Atman	
20.7(31)	Discourse on Atman	
20.8(30)	Discourse on the Field which is the Body	
20.9(30)	Discourse on Subtle Things	

| 20.10(25) | Discourse on the Pure Brahman |

Note- Figure in bracket indicates no. of Ovis

RELEVANCE OF TEACHINGS & WRITINGS OF SAMARTH RAMDAS IN HUMAN RESOURCE MANAGEMENT

D/S/O*	Meaning	HR Concept
2/4/13	It is proper for human body to work for our own welfare and concentrate on the highest goal as per our mite and meditation and offering our belongings.	**Mind Training**
2/9/26-31	Multi tasking, introspective, self-aware, independent of others, discrete, wise, alert in all respects, should not be lopsided, knowledge of physiology and philosophy, aware about path of action, path of knowledge, positive and negative approaches to life, friend to all	**Attributes of Effective Manager**
11/10/25	Mahanta (Leader) should try to groom good people into **Similar capacity,** teach them the strategies and instruct them how to use their intelligence. When they are ready, they should be sent to various parts of the country to handle the work.	**Succession Planning**
11/10/21	Mahanta (Leader) should search many people, know their capacity and they should be taken up in intimate relationship or should be avoided.	**Selection/ Recruitment**

11/10/22	Any work is achieved if there is capacity. If there is no capacity, the work is wasted. Therefore Mahanta (Leader) should constantly assess competence of his people.	**Work Allocation and Performance Assessment**
11/10/23	Mahanta (Leader) should entrust a job to a person, according to his capacity. He should trust a man by examining his worth and activity, at the same time he should keep his prestige intact.	**Work Allocation and Performance Assessment**
12/10/1	We should have reasonable meals and the unconsumed one must be distributed. But to waste it, is not right.	**Waste Reduction**
12/9/29	By using intelligence, you would be as vast as universe. Then what place is there to the faulty pettiness?	**Awareness about Hidden Potential and Talent**
19/10/14	One should not retain the acquired knowledge but should pass it on to others gradually. In that process all will be literate and knowledgeable.	**Education & Knowledge Transfer**
13/10/26	You should teach people as gradually and kindly as one teaches a young child by walking as per the child's speed and being one with its way of thinking.	**Training**

11/9/1	The first part of penance is Duty or action. Our work should be done perfectly. If there is some defect in it, it creates a problem.	**Do it right first time and every time**
14/6/18 & 14/6/19	By wisdom the mind becomes beautiful. The body gets decorated by clothes. Please see what is more important of the two. What do the people benefit by outward show of good garments etc? By cleverness or intelligence many people are protected in many ways.	**Importance of Internal Change**
14/6/6 & 14/6/32	One can overcome ignorance by learning and gaining wisdom. Practical application of the same makes one to understand everything. We should enlighten people by our wisdom but for this acquiring good qualities and virtues is a must.	**Learning and Self Development**
12/2/25 19/8/8 12/2/6	People know how to examine various things but lack introspection and wretchedness follows. The greatest vice is to think that our vice is itself a virtue. This is a great blunder. Right efforts in right direction can bring in fulfillment and success, but people do not understand their own mistakes.	**Self Appraisal**

19/9/22	Organisation has large number of people but they must be strictly controlled. Mahanta (Leader) must behave in a polite way. Consultation will people is desirable but the policy decisions should be taken secretly and secrecy should be maintained.	**Organisational Discipline and Decision Making Process**
19/9/23 & 19/9/24	We must identify wicked persons but should not reveal it and should treat them like treating gentle persons. Otherwise they will be permanent headache. We must attempt to improve them gradually by fondling them when they are found committing wrong deeds.	**Interpersonal Relations**
11/5/20 & 19/9/20	By keeping ego aside, people around us should be assessed. In the event of any mistake from them, they may be kept at a distance but with due care that over a period of time they could join back main stream of improvement. Rusticity must be rigorously dealt with, but with care, that they will not permanently depart.	**Improvement**

11/6/13 & 14/6/31 & 18/10/46	Mahanta (Leader) should know how to act wisely in difficult situations and also to handle various complex problems while remaining aloof himself from danger in those problems. In case a leader decides to go all alone and squabble with others there is a least possibility of his being a successful leader. He influences many people. Organises many Institutions through them.	**Leadership**
19/9/17	If all persons know everything about any work, then the secret will never remain secret and it will leak which may fail the plan. Hence it has to be avoided.	**Secrecy**
2/4/13	Scale higher in life! Realise true nature of self- Atman! Utilise mental and material energies towards the highest goals!!	**Self-Realisation**
5/6/1	Listen carefully the true meaning of knowledge- Knowledge is self awareness! To see one's own self by self is the true knowledge!!	**Knowledge**

18/2/12 18/2/13 18/2/14 18/2/17	You should observe how he behaves tactfully in various situations and study how he gets inspiration. You should follow his alertness and circumspection, his logical thinking and know his ulterior motives even if he does not speak about them. You should study his shrewdness and regularly listen to his thoughts on various subjects. Further you should know how a wise man is very keen and alert, tolerant, generous and learn from it.	**Mentor-Mentee Relationship**

* **Note: - D= Dashaka, S= Samasa, O=Ovi**

RELEVANCE OF TEACHINGS & WRITINGS OF SAMARTH RAMDAS TO MODERN PROFESSIONAL LIFE

D/S/O*	Meaning	Reference
3/4/1	The treasure ways out of the house where number of children are there and therefore begging remains the alternative for meals which will be insufficient.	**Family Planning**
8/2/37	As you develop your determination, you get the results.	**Will Power**
9/4/4	It is the activation of good qualities which make one prosperous and thereby enjoy the fruits of the good deeds. It is beyond doubt that vices lead you to poverty and doom only.	**Discarding of vices**
9/4/13	According to the education and knowledge a man has desires and if there is large enterprise, he gets prosperity accordingly. People generally conduct themselves in the society according to their status.	**Importance of education and knowledge**
15/6/9	One can experience that by proper use of wisdom and hard work even the fate lines on a palm can be changed.	**Efforts superior to destiny**

18/7/7	Those who spend all the earnings, it is very difficult for them to face adverse situations and at times they prefer death over difficult situations. Those who have sound prudence are really wise.	**Money Management**
12/1/1 & 12/1/9	First lead the domestic life neatly and then seek absolute truth with discretion. Do not be lazy and discriminating. One, who exercises caution in domestic life, can only seek divine truth with knowledge. One, who does not lead proper and meaningful life, will not have right divine actions.	**Prapancha and Parmartha**
14/1/63 14/1/64 14/1/65	Do not run after many objects and do not stay at one place too long. One should not overexert himself but indolence is also of no use. Do not be over talkative but too much muteness is also not good. Over eating is not a good thing but to starve is also wrong. Drift into sleep for more than required hours is not a good sign; drift off to sleep is a vice. You should not undertake many vows; but it is also not right to be without any vow or discipline.	**Imbalance in life style**

18/6/7 & 19/6/27	We should avoid excessiveness in all sectors of life and should behave as circumstances demand. A man of discrimination should act according to the situations and should not fall in the pit of adamancy. Do immediately whatever is easy. In case something seems impossible, you can find out the way by wisely thinking deeply.	**Circumstantial Demeanor**
19/9/1 & 18/10/48 & 18/10/50	Wise and detached person having liking for increasing his friends and gathering people around should always go into solitude for some time. Discrimination over the pros and cons of any problem is successful in solitude and in solitude; one can find the way of right effort. In solitude, the thinking becomes so sharp, that logic can reach all subjects in universe. One, who can remain alone successfully, knows everything before others. Such person is great.	**Solitude for Competency**
19/2/2	There are varieties of words, their meanings, various types, thesis and divergence in the word constellations. Communicator should understand all these.	**Effective Communication**

19/2/2 2-23	The most important thing is listening and more valuable than merely listening is thinking about it and understanding it. This leads to satisfaction. We should very shrewdly get information about everything and try to understand their minds.	**Art of Listening**

* **Note: D= Dashaka, S= Samasa, O=Ovi**

CHAPTER 10

Similarity in Teachings and Writings of Samarth Ramdas and Jagad Guru Tukaram Maharaj

Preamble

Maharashtra can amply be termed as place of saints. This place has been and till date fortunate enough to have saints from all castes and creed. The tradition starts from Saint Dnyaneshwar. In the past we have witnessed saints from Brahmin, Maratha, Barber, Carpenter, Goldsmith and Trader communities who sowed the seeds of Bhakti in the soil of mind of people of Maharashtra. They tried to transform Nar (Human Being) to Narayan (God).

1608 was unique year in the history of Maharashtra, which saw birth of two saints in Maharashtra- Rashtra Guru

Samarth Ramdas Swami and Jagad Guru Tukaram Maharaj. Samarth was born at Jamb, did his Sadhana at Takli (Nasik) and his work place was in the region of Krishna River. Tukaram Maharaj was born and brought up at Dehu (Pune).Samarth believed in Lord Rama while as Tukaram's deity was Pandurang (Vitthal from Pandharpur). Samarth initiated Ramdasi tradition while Tukaram belonged to Varkari tradition. Despite this, both taught and wrote same thoughts. Samarth has put it beautifully- "Sadhu disati vegalale! Pari te Swarupi Milale!!("Saints may be seen different but internally they are same")

APPRECIATION OF BEING BORN AS A HUMAN

Table: Samarth Ramdas in Dasbodh (Human Birth)

D/S/O	DESCRIPTION
1/10/1	Blessed is this human body! Please look how wonderful it is! Whatever efforts are done with the help of this body are successful.
1/10/61	If this body is used for search of Truth, the spiritual path, then only it becomes useful, otherwise it is wasted by various calamities on the path towards death.
11/3/1	After many births, this human body is given to us by great luck. Here we should behave morally and with justice.
1/10/18	By the support of this human body many people are liberated by following various paths especially the path of discrimination.
1/10/19	With the help of this human body many attained high status, gave up their egos and remained blissful and happy.

Similar views are expressed by Tukaram Maharaj in Abhang No. 3024 & 4113 in Gatha.

HUMAN BODY: STORAGE OF SORROWS
Table: Samarth Ramdas in Dasbodh (Human Body)

D/S/O	DESCRIPTION
3/1/11	If you see how the body is formed, you will find that there is nothing dirtier than this body because it is formed out of menses.
3/1/18	It is a sack of night soil, smeared inside and out and a bag of urine emanating bad smell.

Similar views are expressed by Tukaram Maharaj in Abhang No. 4113 in Gatha.

FAMILY LIFE
Table: Samarth Ramdas in Dasbodh (Family Life)

D/S/O	DESCRIPTION
14/7/1	There are many types of dresses and many Ashramas (status in society) but the main Ashrama of them is householder's status. In it, all the people in all the three worlds get comfort.
12/1/1	First the family life should be lived nicely. Then the spiritual life should be followed with care. O! The people with good discrimination, you should not be lazy about this latter part.

Similar views are expressed by Tukaram Maharaj in Abhang No. 2085 in Gatha.

DAILY ROUTINE MANAGEMENT

Table: Samarth Ramdas in Dasbodh (DRM)

D/S/O	DESCRIPTION
11/3/17 11/3/18 11/3/22 11/3/24	You should get up early in the morning. There should be washing of mouth, morning bath, Sandhya, prayers, worship of God and offering of food to various hosts of gods. Then you should take your meals or some fruits. Afterwards look after business, trade or whatever duties are there. After dinner you may read something or discuss about some good subject with a friend or two and silently sit alone to read various good books. A blessed wise man does not waste a single moment. He has good knowledge of family duties and business.
11/3/26	You should take part in discussions about religious matters, read mythological books, take active part in the telling of or listening to the story of God and thus do not waste time while doing ordinary work or spiritual work.

Similar views have been expressed by Tukaram Maharaj in Abhang No. 585 in Gatha.

HUMBLENESS
Table: Samarth Ramdas in Dasbodh (Humbleness)

D/S/O	DESCRIPTION
2/7/63	A Sattvic person speaks with humility with all, conducts his life within the norms of social etiquette and gives satisfaction to all people.

Similar views have been expressed by Tukaram Maharaj in Abhang No. 928 in Gatha.

HELPING OTHERS
Table: Samarth Ramdas in Dasbodh (Helping Others)

D/S/O	DESCRIPTION
12/10/5 12/10/6 12/10/7	We should utilise our body in helping others; we should be useful to many people in their work and we should see to it that people do not suffer due to shortages. We should learn about the difficulties and anxieties of others, and help in their need as much as possible. We should talk kindly with everybody. We should be happy by the happiness of others, we should be satisfied and contented by other's contentment and develop hearty friendliness with all, by good words.
14/1/44	You should not fail to help others. You should not harm others. You should not keep doubts in other's mind unclear.

Similar views have been expressed by Tukaram Maharaj in Abhang No. 201 in Gatha.

IMPORTANCE OF EFFORTS
Table: Samarth Ramdas in Dasbodh (Human Efforts)

D/S/O	DESCRIPTION
18/7/3	There is no fruit without hard work. There is no kingdom without hard work. Nothing is achieved without action in this world.
14/1/60	You should not remain without making any effort. You should not even look at laziness. So long as the body is in good condition, you should not leave the practice of spiritual study.

Similar views have been expressed by Tukaram Maharaj in Abhang No. 848 & 159 in Gatha.

DO WHAT YOU SAY! SAY WHAT YOU DO!!
Table: Samarth Ramdas in Dasbodh (Saying & Doing)

D/S/O	DESCRIPTION
12/10/39	People consider as standard, the statements made by that person, who actually makes experiments in his own life and then advices others.

Similar views have been expressed by Tukaram Maharaj in Abhang No. 1399 in Gatha.

ILL FAME
Table: Samarth Ramdas in Dasbodh (Ill Fame)

D/S/O	DESCRIPTION
2/2/41	One should wipe out bad name and earn good name. By discrimination one should hold fast to the path of truth.

Similar views have been expressed by Tukaram Maharaj in Abhang No. 1790 in Gatha.

EQUALITY IN SOCIETY
Table: Samarth Ramdas in Dasbodh (About Equality)

D/S/O	DESCRIPTION
7/2/25	It is not the case that Brahman of Brahmin is sacred and the Brahman of untouchable is polluted. There is no difference there.

Similar views have been expressed by Tukaram Maharaj in Abhang No. 21 in Gatha.

SAINTS

Table: Samarth Ramdas in Dasbodh (Views about Saints)

D/S/O	DESCRIPTION
1/5/16	Saints are abode of joy and happiness incarnate. These saints are the primary source of all contentment.
1/5/17	Freedom finds rest in the saints, they are the fulfillment of the fulfillments, or we can say that they are the fruit of devotion.
1/5/24	The saints give us that gift which is not available in all the three worlds. How can one describe the greatness of such saints?
1/5/26	Such is the greatness of saints and any simile given is inadequate for them, by whose grace the realisation of Paramatman (God) becomes possible.

Similar views have been expressed by Tukaram Maharaj in Abhang No. 676 & 714 in Gatha.

PATIENCE

Table: Samarth Ramdas in Dasbodh (About Patience)

D/S/O	DESCRIPTION
14/1/14	You should not be dejected even though you are insulted and if somebody vehemently criticises you, you should not take it seriously. Even if someone derides you, you should not nurse that insult in your heart.

Similar views have been expressed by Tukaram Maharaj in Abhang No. 25 in Gatha.

IMPOSTOR (HYPOCRITE)

Table: Samarth Ramdas in Dasbodh (About Impostor)

D/S/O	DESCRIPTION
5/2/20	He who freely does anything whatever the mind suggests, and does not observe any discretion is not a Guru. He is just like a beggar, hungry of objects.
5/2/21	Those who do not advise the disciple to do spiritual study, and do not guide him how to control his sense-organs, may be available even three a penny, but such people must be discarded.

5/2/25	That Guru who is subordinating himself to the whims of his disciple is surely the lowest type! He can be termed as robber, a deceptive fellow who is after money.

Similar views have been expressed by Tukaram Maharaj in Abhang No. 708 in Gatha.

REALISATION

Table: Samarth Ramdas in Dasbodh (About Realisation)

D/S/O	DESCRIPTION
19/8/8	The greatest vice is to think that our vice is itself a virtue. This is a very great sin which is a sign of confirmed misfortune.

Similar views have been expressed by Tukaram Maharaj in Abhang No. 2082 in Gatha.

This comparison only proves that both Saint Tukaram and Samarth Ramdas had same views on various aspects of human life and both were preaching same advice to people of their times trying to develop them.

CHAPTER 11

Few Examples of Similarity Between Teachings of Samarth Ramdas Swami and Modern Management Gurus

Tom Peters (Management by Walking Around) suggests that a manager should not be seated in his cabin but take a walk around the plant/office and frequently interact with his teammates.

Ramdas: "Be seated at a place and lose control of all enterprise. Cautiously meet several people." (Samarth expects a good leader to reach out to people instead of staying at one place. He would like him to meet many people, listen to them and comprehend ground realities.)

Stephen Covey (The Seven Habits of Highly Effective People): Proactive attitude is not confined to taking initiative. It means taking charge of our life and make things happen.

Ramdas: With great efforts, one can progress in the spiritual path. There is no solace but to strive hard. Is there anything impossible to achieve without efforts?

Stephen Covey (The Seven Habits of Highly Effective People): "The inside-out approach" says that private victories precede public victories, that making and keeping promises to ourselves precedes making and keeping promises to others.

Ramdas: Ramdas wanted character building instead of superficial transformation. Social change first and foremost warranted individual development.

Shiv Khera- "If you are not part of the solution, you are part of the problem."

Ramdas- Ramdas fought against mindset and countered regressive thoughts. He practiced, what he preached. He took charge of life and tried to solve societal problems.

Stephen Covey (The Seven Habits of Highly Effective People): American self-development literature has been prescribing superficial changes in personality. However the previous literature focused on improving a person's character by promoting values.

Ramdas: In medieval India, Ramdas' focus was similar- character building based on values and principles.

Laurie Beth Jones: People cannot find their missions until they know themselves.

Ramdas: Knowledge is self-awareness! To see one's own self by self is true Knowledge.

Peter Drucker (Practice of Management): Introduced concept of MBO (Management by Objectives) wherein managers set goals for their employees and check their status (Planned versus Actual).

Ramdas: A good leader has to consider five factors while deciding his goal. Considering entire life span, Ramdas suggests holistic planning.

Shamil Naoum: The roles played by a leader and a manager are different. Manager sets targets, establishes standards, encourages development, carries out appraisals, and takes decisions. A leader directs and guides people, influences their thought process, behaviour and ensures goals set are achieved.

Ramdas: His style was focusing on people, inspire trust and he vouched for developing abilities. He was involved in leadership development.

Sherman: "When you boil it down, contemporary leadership seems to be a matter of aligning people towards common goals and empowering them to take the actions needed to reach them."

Ramdas: He challenged status quo of miserable life spent by people in his times and spent time in preparing for the desired social change by empowering common people.

Robert Kenny: "Others see things as they are and wonder why; I see them as they are not and say why not?"

Ramdas: For change, he united people, encouraged learning, ushered people friendly policies and empowered people. Through this route, he brought change. His literature reflects his leadership in thoughts. Ramdas proved to be a great source of leadership.

Jim Collins (Level Five Leadership): A level Five Leader blends extreme personal humility with intense personal will. This refers to the highest level in a hierarchy of executive capabilities. Thus Level Five Leaders are a study in duality: Modest and wilful, humble and fearless.

Ramdas: Ramdas' concept of "people's leader" combines traits of fierce will and personal humility is similar to Jim Collins.

Alleman & Clarke (Mentoring): Only a mentor transfers his insights to a protégée. Mentors, while not a panacea for resolving all problems can help companies deal with a variety of problematic situations. Mentoring can effectively be used to have a bottom line impact.

Ramdas: Ramdas thinks that one of the unwritten tasks of any leader is to have succession planning. The process of identifying right mentor is essential for the success of mentoring scheme.

Stephen Covey (The Seven Habits of Highly Effective People): Habit five- Seek first to understand and then to be understood. Covey says, people do not listen carefully, hence the dialogue remains incomplete and communication gets distorted.

Ramdas: Understand cleverly the minds of others. Why to waste energy without understanding their minds?

Stephen Covey (The Seven Habits of Highly Effective People): Principle of Empathetic communication states that listening and understanding other's mind is very basis of meaningful communication process.

Ramdas: Ramdas bestows great importance on undistorted listening. He says, listening is important but pondering over what others say is still more important. It leads to understanding and satisfaction.

Philips Crosby: Principle of "Right first time and every time."

Ramdas: For zero defects, quality efforts are required.

Leadership Model by Shiv Khera (You can Win)

    a.   Value based positive attitudes

    b.   Avoid ego- the first obstacle in success

    c.   Think and then do.

    d.   Continuous learning

    e.   Hard Work

    f.   Avoid criticism- public humiliation

    g.   Self esteem and confidence

    h.   Inter personal skills and good behaviour

Leadership Model by Peter Drucker

    a.   Organisation Management

    b.   Team Management

    c.   Leadership for Leaders

    d.   Multiple Roles (Mediator, Messenger, Counsellor)

Leadership Model by Ramdas

    a.   Introspection, Walk the Talk

    b.   Knowledge acquisition, self up gradation

    c.   Team Building through delegation, training and development

    d.   Motivation and Inspiration

    e.   Succession Planning

    f.   Organisational Development

This similarity only underlines that the thought process of Samarth Ramdas was ahead of his time and is in line with some of the modern management gurus.

CHAPTER 12

Linkage Between Saints and HR

The works of Ramdas are widely studied by many scholars. He composed his writings in thirteen languages, including Urdu. His literature has been published in ten languages. According to June 1986 issue of "Sajjangad", (Mouthpiece of Samarth Seva Mandal, Satara) 17 scholars from various Universities have carried out research and got their Ph. D. on various aspects of literary work of Samarth Ramdas. According to March 1983 issue of same magazine, around Twelve Hundred articles have been published on "Samarth Ramdas and his work" during the period 1800 to 1950. More than Four Hundred books have been written on Ramdas not only in Marathi but also in other languages such as Hindi, English, Bengali, Tamil, Gujarati, Telagu, Kannada and Urdu.

When it comes to Bhagvad Gita, it is reported that it has been translated into almost all languages (around 40 languages so far) all over the world and has drawn the attention of scholars, saints and mystics. There are countless commentaries written on the Gita (around Three Thousand) at the present day. It is claimed that there are 118 versions of Gita. Samarth Ramdas himself has quoted that he has referred 17 different versions of Gita while writing Dasbodh and he has given the list.

www.tukaram.com is a multi lingual website in 14 Indian and 8 Foreign Langugages. Saint Tukaram is the only Marathi name whose nine poems from the book "Says Tuka" by Dilip Chitre has been included in the "The Longman Anthology of World Literature- The Early Modern Period "(Vol. C), published by Pearson Longman, New York.

However no research is reported to have been carried out in Human Resource Development.

Conceptual Description of the work

The idea of altruism and welfare of all human beings are the underlined principles of Indian Management i. e. Oriental Management. There is a basic difference between Eastern Management and Western style of Management. "Sarve Sukhinaha Bhavantu" (Let all beings be happy) has been our prayer and basic concept of managing things. Our idea is not use and throw concept of Western Management; which resulted in technological development but created imbalance in society, rise in trade unionisation, strikes, lock-outs, industrial unrest.

Organisations have their own set of problems and issues and they are required to find permanent solutions to them. All management is ultimately man-management. Hence addressing HR issues has become paramount important for survival and sustenance.

No. of HR initiatives have been tried out with or without customisation in Indian Industries. They were partially successful and short-lived, since one size does not fit all.

Traditionally literary work of saints has been confined to religious and or spiritual domains. Although saints know the art of man making, really the researchers have paid attention to relevance of teachings and writings of saints to HR practices in organisations. The research took place in humanities, literature, education and such areas, but HR in the context of Management was not considered.

On personal front we sense and experience positive effects of teachings and writings of saints, the same can be extended to modern professional life. If the problems are home grown, then the solutions can also be from our own soil.

Industrial workforce in Maharashtra is well versed with contribution of Saints to society. The concept is to translate the teachings and writings of selected saints into HR practices and interprete and evaluate the impact.

Theorotical Background

Indian Industrialists should study the practical tips and hints given in our ancient books and try to practice them after due customisation so as to maintain Industrial Harmony. Eastern Management focuses upon emancipation of mankind, social furtherance thereby achieving national prosperity.

The Western Philosophers described management as the art of getting the work done by the work force and thereby to achieve organisational goals. A no. of basic management functions need to be executed to make this happen. In the process, the work force is likely to be exploited. Indian Philosophy has a human face and the main intention is Welfare of Mankind.

Human body is like an organisation, working continuously in three shifts. Bhagvad Gita in chapter Six gives importance to the coordination amongst important organs in the human body. In other words, Indian way of looking at Organisation is with development perspective- both Individual as well as organisational development. Western Philosophy gives importance to external behaviour in society and may not be focusing on private life of an employee. On the contrary, purity in private life is of utmost importance to Indian thinkers. Rights are more important in western thinking, while as in eastern philosophy responsibilities are equally important.

The principle of "Yogaha Karmasu Kaushalam" (To perform the job skillfully is a making of one's fortune) is the eastern way of looking at work.

On this backdrop, study of teachings and writings of three saints was decided to check the relevance to modern professional life. Also work related to translating them in HR documents, systems of selected small and medium scale organisations was taken up.

HR Department in any organisation is basically responsible for five important functions:

1. Employment (Entry to Exit of employees)

2. Wage and Salary Administration (Time Office functions)

3. Industrial Relations (Discipline, Communication, collective bargaining)

4. OD Interventions (Training and Development, Career Management, Performance Management System, Potential Appriasal etc)

5. Employee Services and Benefits (Welfare Activities)

The three saints namely Saint Dnyanaeshwar represents Dnyana (Knowledge), Saint Tukaram represents Bhakti (Devotion) i.e- Emotions, while Samarth Ramdas represents Attitude/ Behaviour (Action). Their teachings have focused on positive changes in thoughts and emotions of human beings. Saint Dnyanaeshwar and Saint Tukaram can be considered primarily for Individual Development, while as Samarth Ramdas can be considered both for Individual as well as Organisational Development. "Excellence can only be achieved through Spirituality" was the firm belief of Gurudev Ranade. Bhagvad Gita gives importance to goal orientation, emotion regulation and effective action plan.

While studying human beings in HR function, the three levels are exactly same- Cognitive Thinking (Knowledge Path), Emotive (Devotioal Path) and Karma (Behavioural). Thus HR philosophy of developing human beings is exactly same as the three saints considered for research. Collective study of these three saints can only resemble to HR practices being followed in organisations of modern era. Saints are HR Heads of Society and they are involved in man-making process. In a limited sense HR Department of any organisation has same purpose and objectives. They are also required to offer better quality of life to the employees working in their organisations. Thus taking base of teachings and writings of these three saints in HR policy formulation and employee development initiatives makes sense.

Annexures

1. LEADERSHIP DEVELOPMENT

A manager should possess leadership qualities like focused approach, ability to manage subordinates' actions, proactive and holistic approach, and time management skills. Dasbodh enumerates several leadership principles with focus on character based leadership. The leader does not limit his thinking and is visionary. He is far-sighted and dreams about future. By taking holistic view of any situation, he manages his resources. For Ramdas- a leader has tremendous potentialities but deeply rooted to earth through principles. Decision making is vital to any leadership based on evaluation of options and by carrying out feasibility studies. The consequences of decisions and their after effect on people need to be clearly studied by any leader. Ramdas says leadership is beyond organisational issues and it is way of life. The change process should begin with leader and then only organisational changes can be initiated. According to Ramdas-

1. Leader believes in root cause analysis and disciplined problem solving process.

2. Work allocation in different situations should be strictly as per competence of an individual.

3. Leader tries to avoid conflicts and handles people tactfully.

4. A leader can gain experience by going through variety of situations.

5. Proper time management and avoiding procrastination is must for any leader.

6. Leader must have effective communication skills.

7. A good leader conceptualises and then sets goals.

In **Dasbodh (18/10/46) Ramdas** says; "*A strong and capable leader has to influence many people and get the things done through them using wisdom.*"

A leader is a person who has the ability to direct and guide people, influence their thoughts and behaviour, motivate them and control them to achieve organisational goals.*

Leaders are innovators and by focusing on people, work on status quo. Ramdas practiced various aspects of leadership and preached for development of managerial abilities.

At his math, spread all over India, he appointed Mahantas to spread spiritual teachings, build network, study local situations and then try to bring in changes in the society.

Ramdas believed that the leadership must be goal oriented, efficient, knowledgeable and agile. He wrote letters to rulers highlighting them their functions, duties and responsibilities. According to Ramdas, great leadership acts on what it preaches, thereby winning confidence of people. He keeps people happy and thus succeeds. He is aware of the fact that he has to evolve as an individual by inculcating good habits. Such a leader has to educate people and share knowledge. Thus a leader brings together like-minded, distinctly able people and achieves personal as well as organisational goals. He concentrates on providing solutions to problems without mental agony.

According to Ramdas, any effective leader is strategist. He never shies away from taking guidance from able people. Such leader is dispassionate, balanced, and multi-faceted and solution oriented.

A leader has to scout for talent, motivate people and keep them aligned with organisational goals. He should lead his team from front. Then he is not only effective but also popular. People gather around him to share their joy and sorrows. He is able to read minds of his team members. In Ramdas' words- *A leader should assign work as per the capability and trust people based on their credibility.* His radiating positive energy attracts people. Even if people are upset, he remains calm and composed. Ramdas, like modern management Gurus, emphasised succession planning process.

In crisis, a leader has to prove his metal. Ramdas says; mitigate any critical situation (deadline, resource shortage, tough competition) with more solutions. Preparedness to handle them and coming out of such situation is the characteristic of a good leader.

Mentoring is a process of training, hand-holding of gen-next leaders. A mentor can successfully transfer his wealth of knowledge and insights on various critical issues to a protégée. Ramdas treats this as one of the greatest challenges before leadership. Ramdas has dwelt on how to benefit from the knowledge, experience and wisdom of leaders by protégée. He supported people-centric, character based leadership with long term planning. His Mahantas not only lead in thoughts but also in actions. They visit places, mingle with people to understand their problems and then offer solutions. Ramdas believed that leaders can be developed through active mentoring.

2. GLORY OF MEDITATION

Introduction:

A good virtuous life prepares the mind as a fit instrument for concentration and meditation. Without meditation, one cannot reach self-realisation. It is the only royal road to the attainment of salvation.

Meditation is keeping up of an unceasing flow of consciousness. All worldly thoughts are shunted out of mind. This is the seventh step in the ladder of Yoga.

Yoga is annihilation of all mental functions. This emptying process is difficult one. During meditation, new grooves are developed in the brain and the mind moves upwards in those grooves. When the mind is steady, the eye-balls also become steady. During very deep meditation, the breath does not come out of the nostrils.

Instructions:

You have to meditate now. You have given a definite promise when you were in the womb that you will meditate and realise yourself. You have forgotten your promise. If you practice meditation regularly, a little sleep is quite sufficient. Meditation for a few minutes will give you good sleep later on; meditation itself will refresh you greatly. Keep up the current of meditation while at work also.

If the mind runs towards an object and craves for sense-enjoyment, tell it 'Wait, O Mind! I will give you the bliss of meditation. Please, therefore, O Desire, leave me now.'

You can thus wean your mind away little by little. Once you get real peace and bliss by regular meditation in the early morning, then you will not like to miss a day's meditation. Inner peace comes only as by-product of Meditation.

Meditate now. Meditate a little now and see whether there is such ineffable peace in meditation or not. Close your eyes and meditate on Krishna, Rama, or Jesus, on OM, or your father, or whatever you like.

Chant Om. Taste the bliss of the inner Atman. You should be regular in meditation. Meditate in the early morning; have another sitting after bath; another in the evening; and one more before you go to bed.

If you are poor to have a separate meditation room, set apart one corner of the room you have for meditation.

Every day side by side, along with your duties, practice meditation. This is your foremost duty. This should not be neglected on any account. Get up at 4 a.m. Practice a little bit of meditation and introspect.

Spiritualise all your daily activities. This is very important. Meditating for half an hour in the morning and then doing all sorts of evil actions during the rest of the day will not help you; the Samskaras created by the morning meditation will be wiped out during the day. You must keep up the spiritual current throughout the day.

If you maintain regularity in your meditation, all doubts and difficulties will vanish on their own.

Meditation is related to the seven chakras and the subtle energy system. They are:

1) Mooladhara (Innocence)

2) Swadhisthana (Creativity)

3) Nabhi / Void (Dynamic)

4) Anahat (Confidence)

5) Vishuddhi (Diplomatic)

6) Agaya (Forgiving)

7) Sahastrar (Integrated)

Buddha was asked, "What you have gained from Meditation?" He said, "Nothing, however, let me tell you, what I have lost; anger, anxiety, depression, insecurity, fear of old age and death."

BENEFITS OF MEDITATION

Physiological:

1. It lowers oxygen consumption.
2. It decreases respiratory rate.
3. It increases blood flow and slows the heart rate.
4. Increases exercise tolerance.
5. Leads to a deeper level of physical relaxation.
6. Good for people with high blood pressure.
7. Reduces anxiety attacks by lowering the levels of blood lactate.
8. Decreases muscle tension
9. Helps in chronic diseases like allergies, arthritis etc.
10. Reduction in Pre-menstrual Syndrome symptoms.
11. Helps in post-operative healing.
12. Enhances the immune system.
13. Reduces activity of viruses and emotional distress
14. Enhances energy, strength and vigour.
15. Helps with weight loss
16. Reduction of free radicals, less tissue damage
17. Higher skin resistance

18. Drop in cholesterol levels, lowers risk of cardiovascular disease.
19. Improved flow of air to the lungs resulting in easier breathing.
20. Decreases the aging process.
21. Higher levels of DHEAS (Dehydroepiandrosterone)
22. Prevents, slows or controls pain of chronic diseases
23. Makes you sweat less
24. Cure headaches, migraines
25. Greater Orderliness of Brain Functioning
26. Reduces need for Medical Care
27. Less energy wasted
28. More inclined to sports, activities
29. Significant relief from asthma
30. Improved performance in athletic events
31. Normalises to your ideal weight
32. Harmonises our endocrine system
33. Relaxes our nervous system
34. Produce lasting beneficial changes in brain electrical activity
35. Helps cure infertility

Psychological:

36. Builds self-confidence.
37. Increases serotonin level, influences mood and behaviour
38. Resolve phobias fears
39. Helps control own thoughts
40. Helps with focus concentration
41. Increase creativity
42. Increased brain wave coherence.
43. Improved learning ability and memory.
44. Increased feelings of vitality and rejuvenation.
45. Increased emotional stability.
46. Improvement in relationships
47. Mind ages at slower rate
48. Easier to remove bad habits
49. Develops intuition
50. Increased Productivity
51. Improved relations at home and at work
52. Able to see the larger picture in a given situation
53. Helps ignore petty issues
54. Increased ability to solve complex problems

55. Purifies your character
56. Develop will power
57. Greater communication between the two brain hemispheres
58. Respond more quickly and more effectively to a stressful event.
59. Increases ones perceptual ability and motor performance
60. Higher intelligence growth rate
61. Increased job satisfaction
62. Increase in the capacity for intimate contact with loved ones
63. Decrease in potential mental illness
64. Better, more sociable behaviour
65. Less aggressiveness
66. Helps in quitting smoking, alcohol addiction
67. Reduces need and dependency on drugs, pills pharmaceuticals
68. Need less sleep to recover from sleep deprivation
69. Require less time to fall asleep, helps cure insomnia
70. Increases sense of responsibility
71. Reduces road rage

72. Decrease in restless thinking
73. Decreased tendency to worry
74. Increases listening skills and empathy
75. Helps make more accurate judgments
76. Greater tolerance
77. Gives composure to act in considered constructive ways
78. Grows a stable, more balanced personality
79. Develops emotional maturity

Spiritual:
80. Helps keep things in perspective
81. Provides peace of mind, happiness
82. Helps you discover your purpose in life
83. Increased self-actualisation.
84. Increased compassion
85. Growing wisdom
86. Deeper understanding of yourself and others
87. Brings body, mind, and spirit in harmony
88. Deeper Level of spiritual relaxation
89. Increased acceptance of oneself

90. Helps learn forgiveness
91. Changes attitude toward life
92. Creates a deeper relationship with your God
93. Increases the synchronicity in your life
94. Greater inner-directedness
95. Helps living in the present moment
96. Creates a widening, deepening capacity for love
97. Discovery of the power and consciousness beyond the ego
98. Experience an inner sense of Assurance or Knowingness
99. Experience a sense of Oneness
100. Leads to enlightenment

3. INTERPERSONAL RELATIONS & CONFLICT MANAGEMENT

Gita says- Those who are in Sattva go high in evolution, those who are Rajasik stay where they are and those who are Tamasik go downwards in evolution.

Managing people is essential and unavoidable at all levels of management. People are key to management. No single method can be effective in case of all people as they are different in various aspects. People behave differently at different times and also in different situations. Hence it is essential to identify people around us working in the organisation by predominant characteristics that they possess. This makes man-management easier and simpler, also the conflicts can be reduced to a great extent, if we treat people as they deserve. The three characteristics (Gunas) which constitute Human Nature are SATTVA, RAJAS & TAMAS.

Sattva is light. Rajas is action. Tamas is darkness.

There are four kinds of people. These are- Seer, Sattvik, Rajasik and Tamasik.

Tamasik operate at body level and have physical needs. Their actions are forced and limited. Tamasik see little and do little. The characteristics of Tamasik people are that they are wheel barrows- move as far as pushed, need instant returns. They never own mistakes. Another thing is that, such people need constant supervision.

Rajasik is action oriented and needs ego massaging. These people work at mind/ feeling level. Their actions are forceful. Rajasik does and moves. Such people work for appreciation and can exceed targets. They believe in rework for correcting their mistakes. Rajasik people need periodic supervision and guidance especially for non-routine complex organisational problems.

Sattvik is oriented towards knowledge and needs to be appealed at intelligence level. Their actions are specific and appropriate. These people only see and do. These people are self-starters and work independently. They believe in on-time completion of tasks and these are normally error free. However such people need little supervision.

Seer is insightful and operates at conscious level. Actions of Seers are perfect and practical. They are witnesses and can visualise. Seer take complete responsibility and sets examples. Hence these are respected by Superiors.

Tips and Hints for interacting with people of above categories-

A) Tamasiks

Give them focus and direction. Emphasis on objects is needed. Check their understanding of issues. They need exposure to new situations for updation.

B) Rajasiks

It is important to check whether the directions and focus given are correct or not. Also support in terms of advice needs to be given. The interactions should highlight areas that are likely to be ignored so that complete picture is portrayed. Also constant interactions are needed for identifying opinions and reduction of biases and prejudices. Retention needs to be checked periodically. Finally healthy discussions and debates are welcome for revision and addressing variances.

C) Sattviks

We need to seek summary of impressions about objects and situations. Exchange of ideas/ views is essential to review thoughts. It is important to listen to these people and speak with them openly. Sharing, offering and receiving is a better option while dealing with such people.

D) Seers

We need to approach these people with reverence and request for clarity to get insights about the objects and situations.

There are popularly four methods of managing these people- Sama (persuasion), Dama (reward), Bheda (Discrimination) and Dand (punishment). Sama is treatment as equal, discussions, reasoning, reflection of good will and friendly approach. Dama is appreciation, awards, doing good deeds, giving material benefits, giving money. Bheda is challenge, comparison, unequal treatment, harsh talk, showing dislike. Dand means reprimand, criticism, imposing fines, taking away/ withdrawing facilities, restrictions, rough talk and anger (showing displeasure).

For persuasion Sattvik deserves consulting and participation. Rajasik needs information and guidance. Tamasik needs instructions.

For reward, Sattvik deserves recognition and respect. Rajasik requires power. Tamasik needs incentives and facilities.

For discrimination Sattivk derserves silence. Rajasik needs challenge and Tamasik needs criticism.

For punishment, Sattvik deserves only reprimand and monitoring. Rajasik requires warning and control. While as Tamasik needs restrictions.

In nutshell for man-management examine people working for you in these categories. Effective leadership has to confirm to situations of Sattvik and sometimes to the situations of Rajasik and avoid to the extent possible behaviour of Tamasik. Anger should be a rear resource. It is used only in case of Tamasik as punishment. Even for Sattvik, we need an observer representing pure quality, judgment and overseeing. Bulk of work in any organisation is done by Rajasiks. They need to be managed appropriately. Tamasiks need close supervision.

Sattvik manager uses persuasion and reward regularly and discrimination /punishment judiciously. He normally achieves results and is liked by all.

Rajasik manager uses reward as well as punishments to achieve organisational goals. He is liked by some and disliked by some.

Tamasik manager uses punishment and discrimination regularly. He is disliked and feared.

4. ANGER MANAGEMENT

Anger defeats our sense-organs. Angry person temporarily looses glow on the face, since it underlines inherent weakness present in a person. J. Krishna Murty says "Anger detaches us from others. It makes us temporarily forget all relations and contacts. Anger has some component of strength as well as frustration. People enjoy anger as it provides them outlet to their inner feelings."

Saint Tukaram says, *"Shwan sheegrah kopi, Aapana Ghatkar Papi!"* (Meaning- A person, who gets quick anger, is responsible for his own defeat." Wise people prefer to be away from such angry people. Anger is a two-way weapon. The person who gets angry afterwards regrets his actions taken during that state of mind. The other one who is hurt also gets upset. If you have anger in you, separate fire is not needed. Anger and ego are inseparable friends.

The origin of anger is frustration resulting out of non-fulfilment of expectations. Whenever we are angry, we have one of these feelings- Excitements, helplessness, jealousy or embarrassment.

Things that can lead to angry outbursts are-

Taunts, guilt, protectiveness, combined effects of medication, alcohol and additives, critical comments, displacements, threats, triggered memories, fear of rejection, misunderstandings and feelings of shame, worthlessness vulnerability and inadequacy.

Physical effects of anger:

It has been scientifically proved that anger results into damage of body through a chain of internal reactions- As anger rises; the hypothalamus in the brain stimulates the pituitary glands. These glands release flight or fight hormones, which affect the cardiovascular system and other organs. Hearts start beating faster, blood pressure and body temperature starts rising as lungs struggle for more oxygen intake. Sugar (Glucose) is released in blood to provide extra energy. Blood gets diverted to limbs (to fight) and towards the brain (to think rapidly.) If the anger does not subside, it can lead to stress, anxiety, stomach ulcers, high blood pressure and even heart disease. Hence proper channeling of these feelings is a must.

Chapter Two, Shloka 63 of Bhagvad Gita has a beautiful description of this process. It reads like this-

"From anger arises delusion, from delusion confused memory, from confused memory loss of reason, and from loss of reason one perishes!"

[Meaning- When a person broods over the objects of senses, he develops attachment for them. From such attachment lust develops and that lust is the source of anger. When desires flare up with attachment, anger establishes quickly. Thoughtlessness and indiscretion follows it.]

Therefore one should jettison material desires altogether from the mind, which will automatically destroy attachment and aversion. Then even if the senses indulge into pleasures thereof, they will not be harmful.

Anger is like spark fallen on firewood. So even if thought of material objects occur in mind, it invites such down fall. **(Dnyanaeshwari- Chapter Two, Ovi 329-330)**

Samarth Ramdas in Dasbodh, (Dashaka 2) while sighting signs of fools, calls a person fool, if he is angry and has no courage. If someone gets angry, if slightly insulted and becomes wicked is also a fool.

However anger is never automatic. It has many stages like anxiety, depression, and guilt. In the first chapter of Bhagvad Gita, description of despondency of Arjuna is like this-

"My limbs become feeble, my mouth goes dry, there is tremor in my body and my hairs stand on an end. The Gandiva bow has slipped from my hand, my skin burns all

over, I am not able to stand firm and my mind seems to reel." **(Shloka- 29, 30)**

This is hypothalamus. All these symptoms indicate that Arjuna is stressed. This is true during examinations, interviews and inspections.

In the same chapter **Shloka 38-46** describe Arjuna's agitation and violent grief and clearly indicate that he is angry with self. Anger is blind feeling which leads to self defeating behaviour.

Chapter three, shloka 36 of Gita, says mental agitation is personal property. We are responsible for our anger, whether we like it or not.

The answers are with us only. If we can expel all thoughts of sense-objects from our mind, then passion and hatred are stamped out so there is no harm. A person can remain indifferent to the sense objects, when he is free from desire and anger and is engrossed in the bliss of self.

"The man who forsakes all desires and goes about free from craving, possessiveness and pride attain to peace." **(Gita-2.71)**

The key to anger management is Knowing self (accept what you cannot change, and change what you cannot accept), organising self. Nobody can make us angry without our permission.

Some Tips and Hints-

a) Complete important tasks before they become urgent.

b) On committing mistakes, learn from them rather than loosing cool.

c) Don't criticise, condemn or complain.

d) Never reply to a letter when you are angry.

e) Do not keep eye on erring employees (at work place) or children (at home) that makes you angrier.

f) Meditation- remedy of anger, tension, worry and frustration.

g) *Like a turtle go in your shell for some time.*
   (Dnyanaeshwari- Chapter Two, Ovi- 352)

h) Laughter therapy.

i) Eat RIGHT.

j) SLEEP well.

k) Learn to RELAX.

l) Know your feelings and start writing them.

m) Learn to FORGET and FORGIVE.

n) J. Krishna Murty advices not to store anger. If it is not stored, then we do not need qualities such as forgiveness and compassion. Let us not forget, for every minute of anger, there is loss of sixty seconds of happiness.

5. SPIRITUALITY IN HRM: RELEVANCE TO MODERN PROFESSIONAL LIFE

According to Dictionary, the word spirituality means "the quality of being concerned with religion or the human spirit."

However, there are different interpretations of the word by different people. Some associate it with God, while some others consider it a state of mental peace and happiness. Whatever the interpretation, spirituality is a clear process to develop a sense of morality and ethics within oneself, which helps the individual to be stable and correct during interpersonal transactions.

Gurudev Ranade firmly believed that **"Excellence is possible only through spirituality."**

According to management gurus, basically there are two reasons for this increased interest in spirituality. First the employees' need for meaningful existence are gaining increasing importance. People are looking for more meaning not only in their personal but also professional life. Second, corporate leadership is looking for newer ways to motivate employees and provide innovative solutions.

Need:

Despite of the fact that man has conquered distance and time, despite of the fact that we have ocean of knowledge and far reaching technological advances, still spiritual life is absolutely indispensable and it is the centre of human life. The reason is we continue to face age-old problems. Spiritual life is the one and only solution of all unsolved problems. Over and above these, there are certain man-made problems as well. This has forced human society to live in a world of fear psychosis. Modern man is anxiety-laden creature. The world is full of problems, complexities and there is such a great state of worry, fear and uncertainty that man has started depending on medicines excessively. The greatest of all fears is "Will we survive?" & "Have we future?"

Due to advancement in all walks of life, human beings have acquired global destructive potential.

Why are we not better off than our stone-age ancestors? We have more comforts; life can be easily spent, less exertion. Still there is hostility, hatred, conflicts and restlessness. What is the reason behind this? Is it really the civilisation, in the sense of the word?

The root cause is, man has ignored his nature, spiritual dimension of his personality and is not cultivating the spiritual aspect of life. The outer environment has been drastically transformed. But this materialistic view of life has caused all the problems.

The vision of saints was diagonally opposite. They had realised that human beings have a different identity. Mere ability to think, feel and reason does not alone make man superior to animal in any way. They clearly insisted that unless man is endowed with Sadachara (Good Conduct), Virtue and Dharma (Not religion here, but in the sense of duty), the intellect may cause downfall and result in degradation of human beings. Training should be given to cultivate divine principle- the innermost truth to address this decline. Since the entire attention and focus is on exteriors, the man is unaware of his inner divinity. Essence of education and training is to bring about nobility, awaken the sleeping and slumbering divinity. Comfortable material life alone is no way solution to mankind.

Spirituality brings in compassion, ability to be in the moments of joy and sorrow of others. The greatest virtue in life is Paropakara (doing good to others.) Essence of humanness is making others happy. Understanding that whatever is unpleasant and painful to oneself is equally unpleasant and painful to others is the solution. This is essence of life- knowing inner worth of self. This transformation is evolution. The realisation that "I am inside a spiritual being and I must make use of this phenomenon called life in order to bring about the development of my spiritual self" is the beginning. The western philosophy is geared up only in providing man the necessities for his physical and psychological personality levels and spirituality has taken a back seat. It is necessary to rectify this error. Man now is enslaved and is under control of lower propensities such as passion, anger, greed, sensuality which has made the problem worst. His exterior may be human but the internal nature has become animal.

What we experience at personal level is equally applicable at organisational level, since an organisation is made up of human beings. Hence spirituality in management has become a buzz word these days. A number of factors have brought spirituality to the center stage of discussions. A few of them are:

- Corporate downsizing and retrenchment
- Luxurious lifestyles
- Balancing personal and professional life.
- Materialistic business approach.
- Role conflicts

Besides these, spirituality has gained importance because of the problem of survival in this hyper-competitive world, where growth of education, social upliftment, etc. is common feature. Employees no longer are happy with professional success or material gains alone.

Solutions:

The techniques of attainment or for that matter practice of spirituality may be different, but all of them aim at the same goal, that is, to awaken your inner self, to justify your way of work and to make you mentally and morally fit, so that you give off your best to the organisation to accomplish the organisational goals. Some popular tools of spirituality being used now-a-days are:

- Vipasaana : Silent meditation
- Transcendental Meditation
- Pranayama
- Sudarsana Kriya
- Practice of Raja Yoga
- Siddha Samadhi Yoga (SSY)

Need to Spiritualise the Workplace:

- Recognising Divinity (Spirit) in all beings will make us a Complete Human. (Body-Mind-Intellect-Spirit)
- Spiritualising Economics will reduce Friction.

- Making the Spirit (Divine) work will brings Conviction and Consistency in all operations, acts & decisions.
- Spiritual Leadership & Realised set of Workers (Followers) will lead the organisation towards World Class Excellence.
- Will ensure Survival, Growth & Prosperity in these never before difficult times.

Is spirituality really being practiced? The answer is simply 'yes'. Spirituality has the power to obtain the desired results and to minimise human relations problems' hence; it is gaining priority nowadays among professionals as well as academicians.

It will not be wrong to state that spiritual methodologies have been considered as the last hope by business and professions to tackle all problems. In this era of cut-throat competition, survival is possible only for companies and businesses which are spiritual, besides being professional.

Thus, today, spirituality is an integral part of every business activity. Buzz words such as TQM, MBO and JIT, are being replaced by phrases, such as Aham Brahmasmi and Tat Tvam Asi. For young managers the Bhagvad Gita, the Mahabharata, the Panchatantra and the Vedas are the new encyclopedia for management.

More than 120 companies in India have tie-ups with Maharashi Mahesh Yogi's Meditation Courses to revitalise their work force. A study by the All India Institute of Medical Sciences (AIIMS) shows that regular practice of Sudarshan Kriya and Pranayama increase the flow of positive emotions. The Mount Abu based Brahamakumaris teach regularly the value of listening, tolerance, adaptability and decision making through the practice of Raj Yoga to corporate personnel.

Leading companies are using the principles of social responsibility and good corporate governance. While some are considered to be highly conscious of social and environmental problems, some others are practicing ethical standards.

The age-old wisdom of the Indian seers seems to have caught on today in the world of management. It will only be a reclaiming of our heritage if we in India return to our spiritual lineage and reshape it, if need be, to suit the present claims. It is apparent that we are well placed to take advantage of this knowledge economy, owing to our celebrated spiritual heritage. Indian spirituality is waiting in the corporate corridors ready to serve the business community. The need is for an awareness of it.

Spirituality now is something more than simple meditation and yoga. It is the art of relieving stress and mental hazards.

As rightly said by Prof. S. K. Chakraborty, Indian Institute of Management, Kolkata, "Industry is boldly mining the depths of Indian Wisdom, the Vedaas, the Upanishads and the Puranas, looking for a frame work springing from Indian roots and thought. It is time we rediscovered our own ethos and cultural context if we are to give meaningful and relevant management skills to the youth of the nation."

Results:

Spiritually better evolved people achieve better results. In fact, spirituality may well be the ultimate competitive advantage.

Studies have proved time and again that by implanting the concept of spirituality at the work place tremendous successes can be achieved. It is nothing but a process of acknowledging that people come to work with more than their bodies and minds; they bring individual talent and unique spirits.

One such example is Polyhydron Private Limited, Belgaum, having integrated spirituality into Business Procedures and have gained excellent results.

From this success story we can certainly infer that spirituality at the workplace is an idea whose relevance is being realised more and more.

6. GOAL SETTING

Any task, smaller or bigger, simpler or complex needs proper planning. Planning is nothing but "Thinking before Doing." It is always better to plan so as to achieve objectives. In institutional as well as individual life, planning becomes critical to achieve optimum results in a limited period of time. Today's competitive business environment makes this process very vital.

"Failing to Plan means Planning to Fail." If we decide to face the situations in life, as and when they come and are never ready with necessary home work, we not only waste our energy and resources but also are likely not to achieve our goals.

Samarth Says-

"(Those who) consume all (that they have) earned, they will perish in the difficult times! (Those who) act viewing longer period (in their minds), they are the sensible ones!!

It's not true that the process of planning eliminates all obstacles, one may come across at the time of implementation, but it at least prepares you better for tackling the hurdles.

According to Samarth Ramdas, five factors should be kept in mind while setting goals-

1) **Identification of self-interest** – After taking stock, one has to prioritise the tasks. These need essentially to be aligned with those of organisational priorities. Samarth says- "Scale higher in life! Realise the true nature of your self- Atman!!

2) **Individual Needs-** Goals are linked with individual needs and aspirations. Ramdas says- "Preserve what you have! And gain further going forward!!

3) **Plan period-** Organisations divide financial year in four quarters, plan for each of them and continue monitoring and review process. Individual goals can also be 'short term", "medium term" and "long term."

4) **Resources-** Look at resources required vis-à-vis available at disposal. Ramdas says- "The education will guide the ambition! The enterprise will generate the wealth!! (These factors) in turn will peg the status! As people praise (achievers)!

5) **Will-Power-** This is the true differentiator. Both Abraham Lincoln and Barack Obama are the examples of people who despite their humble background, pursued and achieved higher goals. We

must employ our will power to convert our difficulties into easy actions. Samarth suggests- "As you develop your determination! You see the (commensurate) result!!

Peter Drucker in his "Practice of Management" (1954) underlined the concept of 'MBO- Management By Objectives." In typical Performance Management System (PMS), the organisation decides objectives for its employees and gauge them on the basis of Planned x Actual at pre-determined intervals. However according to Drucker- "MBO works only if you know the objectives." Any good organisation in its Performance Management System starts with goal setting. The goals must be SMART (Specific, Measurable, Achievable, Realistic & Time-bound).

Samarth's advice is replete with tips that throw light on his emphasis on MBO.

Key to success-

a) Identify priorities.

b) SMART goals.

c) Goal- Time frame.

d) Plan of action to achieve/realise goals.

e) Tracking through monitoring and review process.

f) Goals must be "**Moving**". They can be revisited and modified, if needed, based on reviews.

g) Put in the best efforts and succeed.

Above six sample annexures only prove that teachings and writings of saints are relevant to modern HR practices and if such course material is shared with participants during training programs, it can certainly serve the purpose. Professionals today are likely to accept it and practice it, if they find substance and solutions to their problems.

Validation

In order to validate the relevance of teachings and writings of saints to HR, a no. of organisations, both from Manufacturing and Service sector were chosen. Pilot study of their prevalent HR practices was carried out and their HR issues were identified, based on observations and interviews.

The methodology used was-

Approach + Deployment= Results

Based on HR issues, a no. of customised HR initiatives was devised to suit the work culture, organisation climate, and management philosophy of each organisation. The work of saints, their messages from teachings and writings were translated into modern HR practices. The documentation was done and course material for employee training was developed in local language. References were primarily taken from Shrimat Bhagvad Gita, Dnyaneshwari, Tukaram Gatha and Dasbodh.

For a period of about three years, this was tried, tested, at times modified and then finally validated. The results in following areas were visible-

- Employee recruitment process and retention
- Absenteeism reduction
- Leaving of bad habits
- Waste reduction
- Productivity improvement
- Better interpersonal relations
- Improvement in housekeeping levels
- Practicing Yoga, Pranayama, meditation
- Better personal life.

This validation varied from organisation to organisation, but improvements were quantifiable and sustainable. The efforts got strengthened by follow up visits thereby the managements and HR teams of these organisations admitted the improvements and started reaping the benefits. Employees also confirmed positive changes after implementation of new initiatives.

www.ingramcontent.com/pod-product-compliance
Lightning Source LLC
Chambersburg PA
CBHW021814170526
45157CB00007B/2586